The
Next
Archaeology
Workbook

The Next Archaeology Workbook

Nicholas David
&
Jonathan Driver

with contributions by
Steve Daniels
Michael Jez
Pamela Bowyer
Curtis Runnels
&
Sally Stewart

UNIVERSITY OF PENNSYLVANIA PRESS
Philadelphia

upp

Library of Congress Cataloging-in-Publication Data

David, Nicholas, 1937-
    The next archaeology workbook/Nicholas David & Jonathan Driver:
with contributions by Steve Daniels . . . [et al.].
        p.   cm.
    ISBN 0-8122-1293-2
    1. Archaeology--Handbooks, manuals, etc. 2. Archaeology-Problems, exercises, etc.
I. Driver, Jonathan C. II. Title.
CC75.7.D38   1989   89-40406
930--dc20   CIP

Contents

Acknowledgments

First, we thank Steve Daniels for his legacy, and for his contribution of the *Kufungua* problem. Thanks also to Michael Jez, Pamela Bowyer, and Sally Stewart, all graduates of the course based on the first Workbook at the University of Calgary, whose final assignments have now blossomed into print. Curtis Runnels, who teaches archaeology in innovative ways at the University of Boston, kindly contributed *The Neolithic of Arak*. In devising the remaining problems we have drawn on the writings of colleagues too numerous to mention, but should implicate Judy Sterner, whose ethno-archaeological fieldwork in Cameroon inspired the *Khina* problem and whose Master's thesis was important in producing *Cuimayo*. We also thank Anne Katzenberg, Jane Kelley, Ian Kuijt, Yvonne Marshall, and John Topic for ideas and criticism. Erle Nelson gave us invaluable advice, all of which we took, on the tricky matter of radiocarbon dating.

Thanks also to the illustrators for the imaginative efforts and skills that add a great deal to many of the problems. Eva David contributed Figures 1.2 and 2.1 and calligraphy. Bob Birtch of the Instructional Media Centre (SFU) did the drawings for *Repton, Little Bison, Earp County,* and *Cook Valley;* Andrea Lawrence for *Barchester;* Willa Ingelson for *Latreia, Cuimayo,* and various maps. A grant from the Simon Fraser University Archaeology Department assisted in the production of many figures. Jonathan Driver thanks Cathy, Simon, and Andrew for sharing the fieldwork on which certain of these exercises are based.

Last but not least, students at the universities of Boston, Calgary, Simon Fraser, and Stanford have worked through earlier drafts of these data sets and deserve a generous measure of credit for their hard work and thoughtful comments.

A Preface
for Instructors

This book is not a *New Archaeology Workbook;* nor, alas, do we feel justified in entitling it *Contextualizations in Post-Processual Epistemology,* which might impress an unwary Dean. It is merely the ***Next*** *Archaeology Workbook,* successor to *The Archaeology Workbook* by Steve Daniels and Nicholas David (Philadelphia: University of Pennsylvania Press, 1982). The goal of this sequel, one would hope not the archaeological equivalent of *Evil Dead II,* remains the same as that of its predecessor—to encourage students to sharpen their analytical skills by applying their knowledge of archaeological theory and method to data resembling those encountered in archaeological reports from around the world, but which are here more conveniently packaged. Those who have used simulations, whether those of the previous Workbook or of their own devising, for teaching or learning archaeology have found them an effective preparation for the analysis of "real" data.

This book contains an entirely new set of problems suitable for students in the second and later years of a Bachelor's degree in archaeology, and for senior undergraduate and first year graduate students who have come up through anthropology or other programs in which archaeology is only one of a number of subdisciplines. The parameters are otherwise unchanged, and this preface and the introduction for students that follows repeat, with modifications and changes in emphasis, much that was in the previous book. Thus, this book might profitably be used in conjunction with the previous one, if a larger number of problems is desired for the purposes of a particular course.

As is implied above, the *Workbook* is designed for students with a grounding in archaeological theory and method. That is to say, they have worked their way through a good introductory text and have been exposed to basic concepts, to discussion of the nature of the archaeological record and of the importance of context, and to the most commonly used methods and techniques for the collection and analysis of data. They are aware that classification makes comparison possible and that the particular approach employed should be attuned to the problem under study. Stratigraphy is not a closed book to them; they can read simple sections. They can draw inferences from distribution maps. Students should also be familiar with simple economic, ecological, and chronological reasoning based on evidence from geology and the life sciences, zooarchaeology in particular.

We expect some understanding of the theory and practice of relative and absolute dating, and hope for, but rarely find, a critical understanding of isotopic dating methods, their probabilistic nature, and the factors affecting their reliability. Calibration of radiocarbon dates, including correction for differential fractionation, poses difficulties that will require some class discussion besides the limited information offered students on page 11 below. In some problems we have provided calibrated dates, in others dates in the standard format calculated according to the 5568 half-life and corrected for fractionation. Unless it is wished to make a special point of investigating the effects of calibration on chronology, we suggest that students be advised to assume, for present purposes only, that calibration would not significantly modify the chronologies based on uncalibrated dates.

Although the problems are set in various parts of the world and in different periods (with appropriate local color), students need not know the details of areal prehistory. They cannot improve their interpretation of the data contained in these exercises by consulting more and more site reports and regional syntheses. Instead they must exercise their ingenuity and knowledge of archaeological principles. Local technicalities and jargon, where not avoided altogether, either are comprehensible in the context of the problem as a whole or are included in order to encourage students to engage in a little library research. A previous acquaintance with the outlines of world prehistory or those of a major culture area does, on the other hand, help to provide an understanding of the kinds of explanation and reconstruction most commonly offered. We have attempted to order the problems so that they become progressively more difficult through the book, but it should be realized that the degree of difficulty depends in part upon the students' previous training and on the instructor's briefing.

A wide but limited range of issues is addressed. Most problems require students to develop a culture historical sequence, either as the goal of the exercise or as a necessary step toward it. Numbers 1, 2, and 4 are relatively simple exercises in culture historical reconstruction using varying combinations of stratigraphic, distributional, typological, chronometric, faunal and human biological, linguistic and historical evidence. In each the student is asked to construct an outline culture history of a little known region and to identify the underlying culture processes. *Repton Barrow,* another problem appearing early in this book, is narrowly focused on the history of use and abuse of a single site. *Barchester,* based on excavations in British urban contexts, is a more complex exercise in the unraveling of stratigraphic and architectural data.

As a reflection of changing emphases in archaeology over the past decade, hunter-gatherers, among them complex foragers, receive more prominence in this volume than in the last, with the *Little Bison* and *Cook Valley* problems being largely devoted to them. The latter exercise, the last and most demanding in the book, deals with successive socio-economic transformations. In *Earp County,* the student is invited to infer the relationships over time between settled Puebloans and their bison-hunting neighbors on the Plains.

The *Latreia* problem is concerned with the criteria for the recognition of ritual behavior in the archaeological record. While also involving ritual, the ethnoarchaeological *Khina* exercise is more generally concerned with the implications for archaeology of a variety of cultural transformation processes. *Cuimayo* is an exercise in research design for the simultaneous testing of multiple hypotheses. Experience has indicated that such problems are best administered after students have had considerable experience in solving others in which the research design is a given. And lastly, since ethical and political dilemmas are now explicit and unavoidable in almost all areas of archaeological endeavor, we have included *Golden Ears Rock* as an introduction to such quandaries.

As in the previous book, and as in the data sets that we deal with from day to day, the evidence presented is incomplete and of varying and often doubtful validity (including the odd error), and may on occasion not be strictly relevant. Students will gain nothing, for example, from the decipherment of the Linear B tablet in *Latreia* other than some knowledge, worthwhile in itself, of that script. The questions are open-ended; there are no right answers, only constructions of varying levels of plausibility. One of the benefits of tackling such problems is to bring forcefully home to students how often in archaeology a choice between interpretations rests not on the establishment of this or that fact, but on the comparative economy, in terms of our theory-based expectations of human behavior, of two or more arguments. Although the authors of the exercises had particular historical scenarios in mind, students will vigorously propose and occasionally quite successfully defend very different reconstructions.

However ingenious, problems of this kind have obvious limitations as teaching devices. Constraints arise from our attempt to make the problems accessible to a wide range of students, who may or may not be enrolled in formal courses of instruction. We have therefore omitted many lines of evidence that seem to us to require more specialized knowledge. Other data, as from historical linguistics, oral traditions, texts, and faunal and floral evidence, are presented for the most part as givens. Also predigested, or at least premasticated, is the typological evidence, partly because the addition of typological ambiguities would have made our problems too long and complex, but even more because we feel that typological skills and sophistication can best be acquired by handling real objects in the context of real problems, not by looking at pictures on a page.

The emphasis on generality has also led us to omit various specialized fields within archaeology. Industrial and underwater investigations and astro-archaeology, for example, have their own interpretative and procedural problems with which we do not expect the average student to be familiar. Neither does our framework allow us to deal with more than one or two aspects of complex societies at a time. While no problems are explicitly post-processual in theme, this area is touched on in the *Khina* problem. Space has precluded the inclusion in this volume of a historical archaeology data set.

Before they start, students should read the Introduction, as this describes the conventions adopted by the authors and gives advice on approaches to problem solving. In this *Workbook* we have not provided a sample answer to the first problem but instead a partial tabulation of the data designed to set students on the right track. Students obviously floundering may be well advised to contemplate the sample student's and instructor's answers to the *Falasia* problem in the first *Workbook*.

With the benefit of our own and others' experience in using that text, we are better prepared to offer advice to the uninitiated. We strongly recommend that instructors construct answers to problems before assigning them. This allows them to adjust the degree of difficulty to their students' capabilities, either by giving them advice on how the problem should be tackled, or by subtracting from or adding to the instructions at the end of each problem.

Thus, for example, students doing the first, *Kufungua,* problem might be asked to produce tables of pottery percentages that would point to cultural processes different from those that underly the data as presented. In the *Golden Ears Rock* problem, the potential conflict of interest affecting the Cultural Heritage Officer's actions may perhaps be better discussed in class than written into the answers—and so on.

Whatever the frequency with which problems are set, weekly as the main or entire content of a course, or at less frequent intervals, we have found it best if students hand in written answers before any class discussion takes place. We then make a careful choice of one student to present his or her answer to the class for group discussion and criticism. Many students are quite unaccustomed to presenting and arguing ideas in an academic forum, and are at first unable either to marshal arguments effectively or to criticize an inference incisively without wounding its perpetrator. (We have all been to conferences and workshops where professional archaeologists showed themselves woefully unable to distinguish between legitimate criticism of their ideas and personal attack.) Some may attempt to "prove" their point by bullying assertion; others simply keep their mouths shut. Others again fail to recognize when they are beat and, perhaps for fear of losing marks, will defend a lost cause to the point of exhaustion. Practice in reasoned debate makes perfect.

If training in collegial discourse has thus proved an important incidental benefit of these problem sets, the instructor must also be sensitive to students' feelings, giving credit for an interesting or imaginative thought even if it leads to a wrong conclusion. Especial care must be taken not to "put down" students, who are at a status disadvantage even though there are no "right answers" to which the instructor has privileged access. While the instructor is best seen but not heard for most of the class, he or she can greatly improve the learning experience by ensuring that the more bashful or diffident students are heard from, by moving the class on when discussion of a topic is nearing unanimity, and by insisting on the exploration of alternative hypotheses at every stage. The level of argument can also be raised by the judicious introduction of relevant theory and comparative materials.

The class format suggested above is inappropriate for the *Golden Ears Rock* problem. In this case we have found it best to have students prepare written answers as usual, but in addition to assign them (whatever their private opinions) roles to play in class as indigenes, industrialists, or archaeologists in a debate chaired by the instructor as representative of the Gonbwanaland Ministry of Culture. If the students wish to dress their parts, so much the better.

In several courses in which we have worked our way through the *Workbook* and other problems, the students' final assignment has been, whether singly or in small groups, to prepare a problem of their own. Nothing brings home to them more vividly the interdependence of the components of any and all archaeological data sets.

Instructors are warned that some students will expend an inordinate amount of effort in problem resolution, while others will offer only a summary of inferences unsupported by arguments. Composition of answers to problems should not make disproportionate demands on students' time, but it is best to make this explicit and to monitor input as well as output. Few will comprehend that the presentation of data in tabular form is, in most instances, in itself a significant step in their analysis, and one worth taking trouble over. (Others will waste time in the production of beautifully crafted graphics that merely dress up known data, failing to disguise a lack of analytical insights.) Some will be unwilling to synthesize data from particular sites into a regional culture sequence or to group assemblages into phases and cultures. It takes time for them to appreciate that there may well be developments that the archaeologist finds convenient to label as a change of culture, even when there has been no turnover in population. Many will need to be encouraged to present alternative hypotheses, test these with such data as are available, and come to a tentative decision between them. And there are those who, failing to learn from the data, are condemned to repeat it.

Like some distinguished archeologists, students may refer to data in the singular, or misuse the verbs "assume," "infer," "imply," and, less frequently, "induce" and "deduce." Ignoring the nature of the archaeological sample, they will persistently infer that because item X turns up at site Y and later at site Z it must have diffused directly from the former to the latter. And it may be that they will take radiocarbon dates as given by God (or Science)—and the one sigma range of error to represent the duration of the deposition of the layer from which the sample was collected. To paraphrase a Herman cartoon, the frequency with which you find yourself correcting such errors is a pretty good indication of your and your colleagues' performance as teachers.

NICHOLAS DAVID
JONATHAN DRIVER
31 January, −39 B.P.

An Introduction
for Students

For some reason, while students always read the Preface for Instructors, you are less eager to work through information which is specifically directed at you. As a last resort it does pay to consult the manual!

In developing these exercises, their authors first thought of problem areas in which students could gain needed competence through simulations: working out a regional culture history, for example, or learning how to recognize ritual behavior in the archaeological record. Then they decided on a particular plot or structure of events and the processes that brought them about, then on a geographic region in which the events might have taken place. Finally, after consulting the literature for "local color," they fleshed out the plot and transformed it into data such as might have been recovered by archaeologists and specialists in related fields. But this does not mean that you can reverse the process, work backward, and arrive at a solution identical to our original scenario in which groups of people, variously motivated, do different things at different times and places. There are several reasons for this, and they are worth understanding because they apply in real archaeological situations where the plot is provided not by David, Driver, et al., but by God, the force of history, Dharma, Great Men, or the unfolding logic of systemic evolution.

First, and very practically, there is the matter of data recovery. The material manifestations of cultural systems do not simply subside into the ground when their useful life is over; they are transformed into potential archaeological data by both natural and cultural formation processes and *may* then be sampled by an archaeologist, or indeed by a grave robber. Preservation and the intensity of archaeological research vary from region to region, site to site, and even layer to layer. Techniques of recovery are constantly improving; excavators vary in their expertise. Thus in any one area, besides the latest high-powered but still imperfect monograph, you will find scrappy but vital reports of digs carried out in ways that we would now characterize as criminal. The analyst is constantly having to make use of information of uneven quality, even if all the data are drawn from the same "homogeneous" culture.

Second, even in the best studied area, the archaeological data document only a tiny fraction of its past peoples' activities. Many recent developments in archaeological method are aimed at ensuring that this fraction is as representative as possible of the range of past behaviors originally present. Research design is or should be directed toward ensuring that the analyses carried out are efficient, in that they are adequate to solve the immediate problems while not being unnecessarily time consuming or expensive. Neither should they prejudice any further analyses that may foreseeably be required at a later stage in research. Especially in early problems in which you are asked to block out the prehistory of a little known region, the typological and other "predigested" data, on physical anthropology for example, that you will meet with are for the most part pretty basic, as is not unusual in such circumstances. In any one problem we can only provide you with a few sites and a limited range of fossilized activities. Although we have constructed the data so that there are linkages suggesting certain interpretations (as may well not be the case in real life), you should never forget that you are dealing with a small sample subject to unknown biases. Direct connections between any two sites are improbable even if they are the *only* two sites at which a certain phenomenon is known. As you will find when faced with real data, inferences must be made on the basis of inadequate evidence, including others' work that you may consider invalid in whole or in part but which for practical reasons cannot be checked. A good archaeologist learns to accept this and to define areas of ignorance and uncertainty, specifying how these might be reduced by further work.

Third, there are the limitations of archaeological theory. Lewis Binford once wrote that "The practical limitations of our knowledge of the past are not inherent in the nature of the archeological record; the limitations lie in our methodological naiveté, in our lack of development for [he must mean "of"] principles determining the relevance of archeological remains to propositions regarding processes and events of the past."[1] This is an inspiring if overoptimistic view. There are absolute limits to archaeological inference but, Binford is right, we are as yet far from being constrained by them except where they concern matters that are intrinsically insignificant. We are still remarkably naive, and not surprisingly so, since our short life span makes it difficult for us to observe many processes that structure our data, and most archaeologists work with the material remains of cultures they do not and cannot experience directly—even if they do attempt to immerse themselves in relevant comparative materials. Too much archaeological inference is still founded on "common sense," often a complacent term for ethnocentric preconception.

ARCHAEOLOGICAL ENTITIES

In a moment we will tell you about the conventions we have followed in formulating the problems and offer advice as to how to approach them. Before doing so, we should, if not agree on, at least bring to your attention the different sets of concepts used to describe archaeological entities. The British write, for example, of "assemblages," "industries," and "cultures"; French authors of "outillages" or "séries," "industries," and "civilisations", "industries" having a different range of meanings in the two languages. Just as there is no one right typology but a variety of approaches that can profitably be employed at different stages of research, so it is unreasonable to expect that the same analytical concepts will fit both the Mousterian of the Mediterranean basin and the Classic of Oaxaca. In preparing your answers, you will have to choose terms that suit the problem. Although you have probably already been exposed to this aspect of archaeological theory, you may find the two sets of concepts given below to be of some use. They should at least discourage you from thinking and writing about undefined entities such as "the people" or

---

[1] L. R. Binford, Archeological perspectives. In *New perspectives in archeology,* ed. S. R. Binford and L. R. Binford (Chicago/New York: Aldine, 1968), p.23.

even "they." Variants of the first set, extracted with modifications from D. L. Clarke's *Analytical Archaeology* (London: Methuen, 1968) are used by many British writers.

Attribute: a logically irreducible character such as length

Artifact: any object modified by a set of humanly imposed attributes

Artifact type: a population of artifacts that shares a recurring range and combination of attributes

Assemblage: an associated set of "contemporary" artifacts

Culture: a polythetic[2] set of artifact types that consistently recurs together in assemblages

Culture group: a family of related cultures, characterized by assemblages sharing a polythetic range of different varieties of the same artifact types

Technocomplex: a group of much more distantly or unrelated cultures sharing the same general families of artifact types as a widely diffused and interlinked response to common factors in environment, economy, and technology

These definitions obviously raise several questions, for example, the meanings of "contemporary" or "family."

The second set, adapted from G. R. Willey's and P. Phillips's *Method and Theory in American Archaeology* (Chicago: University of Chicago Press, 1958), has the advantage that the archaeological entities are defined with reference to a previously given spatial framework. The time frame may be either relative or absolute, but the duration of specific units or series will depend on rates of culture change.

Spatial Divisions

Site: a variable area (camp to city) more or less continuously covered with archaeological remains that pertain to a single unit of settlement . . . the basic unit for stratigraphic studies. Cultural changes result from the passage of time

Locality: a variable area not larger than the space that might be occupied by a single community or local group and small enough to permit the working assumption of complete cultural homogeneity at any given time

Region: likely to coincide with a major physiographic subdivision in which at a given time a high degree of cultural homogeneity may be expected but not counted on . . . the space that might be occupied by a social unit larger than the community, possibly the "tribe" or society

---

[2] A group is poythetic if each of its members possesses many but not all group characteristics, each characteristic is possessed by many members, and no single characteristic is diagnostic of group membership.

Area: corresponds to the "culture area" of the ethnographer and tends to coincide with major physiographic regions

Basic Archaeological Units
Component: the archaeological materials found in a single level of a single site, the manifestation of a given phase at a single site

Phase: a unit possessing traits sufficiently characteristic to distinguish it from all other units similarly conceived, whether of the same or of other cultures or civilizations, spatially limited to a locality or region and chronologically limited to a relatively brief interval of time

Culture and civilization: reflect the major segments of culture history . . . groups of phases

Temporal Series
Local sequence: a chronological series of components or phases within the geographical limits of a locality

Regional sequence: a chronological series of phases within the limits of a region, arrived at by correlating local sequences

Integrative Units
Horizon: a primarily spatial continuity represented by one or more cultural traits whose nature and mode of occurrence permit the assumption of a broad and rapid spread

Tradition: a primarily temporal continuity represented by persistent configurations in single technologies or other systems of related forms

This abbreviated listing cannot fairly represent Willey's and Phillips's thought; for example, they insist that "the concept of phase has no appropriate scale independent of the cultural situation in which it is applied." This may be taken as generally true of the other entities; the Acheulian cleaver may have taken tens, even hundreds of thousands of years to spread over large areas of the Old World, tobacco pipes only a hundred years or so, but both are used as horizon styles. You may find it useful to make a diagram showing the relationships of the different concepts and to consider whether others might not sometimes be needed. A level may contain materials of varying ages; should these be described as a component? If a community regularly moves between winter and summer camps, fishing in one and hunting in the other, might it not be appropriate to distinguish the resulting components (or assemblages) as "facies" of the same phase? As so on.

Refer again to this section when you attempt the first problem. It is important because in order to think about something you need words or symbols to apply to it. But these words are not tyrants; they are there for your convenience. People may differ in their judgments as to whether the artifacts and their contexts in two assemblages are sufficiently different to be assigned:

- to different cultures (even perhaps if they were made by people related closely to each other biologically), or

- to different phases of the same culture (even perhaps if they are only 50 years apart in time), or

- to the same phase (even if they were made by people of different physical type some 1500 years apart).

Remember that, if other sites had been excavated that sampled different segments of the record, you might well have divided it into cultures and phases quite differently. Archaeologists are constantly redefining entities from attributes on up to civilizations. But if you can say that two assemblages share the same tradition of stone-working and participate in the same technocomplex, but are not of the same culture, your meaning will be clear enough for argument to be possible.

It is quite remarkable that radiocarbon dating has survived as a technique when almost all its critical assumptions have been shown to be false. We have learned that:

RADIOCARBON DATING

- The rate of production of ^{14}C by cosmic ray bombardment is not constant, and not always in balance with its rate of decay. Therefore the concentration of ^{14}C in the atmosphere varies through time.

- ^{14}C does not mix rapidly in all environments, so that, for example, some marine organisms will provide radiocarbon dates older than their actual dates of death.

- Not all living things accumulate ^{12}C, ^{13}C, and ^{14}C in the same relative proportions. They may fractionate it differentially.

- After death the surviving parts of the organism are not closed systems. Under certain circumstances they can exchange carbon with their environment.

- Finally, we have known for some time that the 5568 year half-life is nearer 5730 years.

Fortunately in many cases the differences between reality and the assumptions are minor, and the development of calibration methods (discussed below) has reduced some of these problems. Physicists and some archaeologists have learned to cope with these complexities, but they have made radiocarbon dating more difficult to understand. In this book, radiocarbon dates are presented in two different ways, although within any one data set only one method will be used.

First, as has long been standard archaeological practice, we present radiocarbon dates with a one sigma error (standard deviation), 1500 ±100 B.P. When this format is used, you should assume that the date is corrected for fractionation and that (by international convention) the 5568 half-life has been used. Such dates are in radiocarbon years; they have not been calibrated—no adjustment has been made for irregularities in the radiocarbon curve—and cannot be converted into calendrical dates merely by subtraction from 1950. For the purposes of the exercise, you may assume that calibration would have little effect on the chronology. Remember that a date expressed in this format means that there is a 68% chance that the organism(s) dated died within the one sigma range (in the example above, between 1400 and 1600 B.P.). If two chances out of three seem a poor bet, you can increase the probability to 95% by taking a two sigma range (i.e., 1300 to 1700 B.P. in the example above).

Second, as is becoming increasingly more common, we present calibrated dates. You should be familiar with the concept of calibration (and know that even the calibrated age varies a little depending on whose calibration curve and statistical methods you use!). If not, look it up in a recent textbook. Although some archaeologists express calibrated determinations as a single date (e.g., 1240 cal. A.D.), based on the intercept of the radiocarbon age with the calibration curve, this is incorrect. Radiocarbon ages have associated uncertainties and intercept the calibration curve over a range. If the calibration curve is complex at that age, this can even mean that a single ^{14}C date can be calibrated to two or three calendrical dates. One also has to take into account the standard deviation of the radiocarbon date; the extremes of the sigma range will also produce a range for the calibrated age (e.g., 1170 to 1390 cal. A.D.). Even more confusing, because calibration curves are not smooth, the midpoint of this range will not necessarily be the same as the calibrated radiocarbon date (1240 cal. A.D. in the example above). Phew!

In some exercises in this book we use both calibrated radiocarbon dates and dates expressed in calendar years, for example, tree ring dates or dates based on historical records. In those problems we express the radiocarbon dates in calibrated form in order to make the dates, whether isotopic, dendrochronological, or from documentary sources, as comparable as possible. We give only the calibrated A.D. or B.C. range for the dates, based on the one sigma range of the original ^{14}C date. Thus a date such as "1320–1450 cal. A.D." shows the possible range of calibrated values for the original ^{14}C determination. Unfortunately it is very difficult to work out the probability that the calibrated date lies within this range. It can, however, be assumed that the probability is less than 100%, and that the actual date of death of the dated material probably but not definitely falls within the range given.

Regardless of how radiocarbon dates are calculated, it is important to remember that all a radiocarbon date does is provide an estimate of the time the sample organism(s) died. You have to decide whether it is likely that death coincided with incorporation into archaeological deposits, and whether the remains found in association are likely to have been deposited at the same time.

OTHER CONVENTIONS AND PRACTICAL ADVICE

Let us now get down to cases. You will note that the problems are set in different parts of the world, some of which may be unfamiliar to you. Don't lose heart; only the cultural vocabulary changes, the syntax of archaeology remains the same. You should be able to apply your knowledge of the discipline in any area. We have tried to achieve a degree of verisimilitude in all the problems. Although the settings, events, and materials are fictional, they or others quite like them could have occurred in the location in which they are set. So before starting a problem, feel free but not obliged to consult a secondary source on the archaeology of its area. Although unnecessary, knowledge of the region and period in question will be a help rather than a hindrance, and you will learn a little world prehistory on the side.

You already know that several of the early exercises involve reconstruction of the culture history of an area. This is also true of the *Little Bison* problem; in fact in the majority of the later ones such reconstruction will be a necessary step in coming up with an answer to the specific questions posed. So the advice that follows is of general relevance. You are being asked to do in a small way what was done for you in the first lecture you went to on Mesopotamia or in that chapter on the Andes in the world prehistory text. How do you set about this? First, it is important that you pay attention to all the data given even if, upon reflection, you decide to discard some as irrelevant. The text, tables, and figures supply complementary information and are not there for decoration. After you have studied the data carefully, your next step is to establish a geographical and chronological framework. There is no point in talking about how various events and activities are related economically, socially, or otherwise until you have decided that they were near enough in space and time to have been related at all. Consider the geography. Examine the area, and if possible divide it into regions as defined above. Regions that are ecologically similar but widely separated on the ground are best treated as quite different. Then start to construct the chronology. This is easiest to do one region at a time, and, if there are enough sites, one locality at a time, starting with the site that has produced the finest stratigraphy. The suggested procedure for each region is as follows; refer if you wish to Figure 1.2.

Take a sheet of rough paper and draw vertical time columns for each site, "Late" at the top and "Early" at the bottom, and a summary column for the region. Scale the columns to cover the period under study. Enter at the appropriate points any exact dates for historical events. Then enter estimates, such as radiocarbon dates, using a vertical line to represent the range of each. Do not forget that, quite apart from statistical uncertainty, you should determine whether the samples are likely to be genuinely associated with what they purport to date, and bear in mind that errors can arise from contamination in the field or even faulty procedures in the laboratory. Opposite the dates you can place any economic, typological, climatic, or other information to which the dates refer. When all "absolute" dates are in, information for which there are only relative dates can be added. The time columns, prepared locality by locality, and the region column are now a first approximation to a chronology. If your choice of regions has been good, the chronology of any one region is likely to be fairly simple (that is, of course, if the data are there with which to build it). If you find that closely comparable events occur at very different times in parts of the same region, then your initial choice may have been poor, some dates are perhaps misleading, or you may be dealing with an historical process. Note and mark any discrepancies, but leave making final decisions on them until a later stage.

When you have time columns for each region, they can be compared with the aim of building up an overall framework. If there are no clear groupings of components into phases and of phases into cultures that can be correlated from locality to locality and from region to region, you may find it helpful to subdivide the time span into "periods," a general purpose term conveniently employed in early stages of research. Periods are best chosen so that similar conditions of life prevailed throughout any one, though periods defined only by major or easily recognizable events (the appearance of copper, for example) at the start and finish can also be useful. Periodization depends in part on availability of data; as mentioned above, a different selection of sites for excavation might, and probably would, have suggested a somewhat different scheme.

Major events and periods can be correlated from region to region to produce a connected areal chronology; bear in mind that the dates of particular events may indeed differ from one region to another, for reasons that you are invited to infer. Throughout the process of establishing a framework, you will find discrepancies and contradictions and will have to decide whether these are real and require historical explanation, or are mere artifacts of research, perhaps the consequences of a small or unrepresentative sampling of the range of prehistoric past behavior. If they are real, can you account for the anomaly? Several reconstructions are almost always possible, and thorough checks of each against the details of the evidence are likely to be required before you reach a framework you find convincing. Even then, as with real archaeological problems, loose ends may remain that cannot be explained.

Once you have decided on a framework, it should be much easier to examine each region at a particular period, and to try to group the phases and reconstruct the economic, social, and political system or systems within it. If you think a system is sufficiently homogeneous, you may wish to give it a cultural name, usually based on a "type site" at which it was first recognized or is best expressed. Or again your reconstruction of one aspect may send you back to alter the main time and space framework. You may, for instance, find that some class of artifact is indicative not of a separate culture but of a particular economic activity, or that what you had provisionally identified as a political entity makes better sense as evidence of a trade route. Understanding patterns and processes in the past depends to a considerable extent on your knowledge of comparable patterns and processes documented by prehistorians, ethnographers, and others—including those you observe in your daily life. Do not therefore regard any of the problems as capsules set apart from your other courses and experience; bring all your knowledge into play. And finally, however attractive you find your own reconstruction, you should not accept it wholeheartedly (if at all!) until you have examined alternatives and decided that, for specific reasons, they are definitely less satisfactory. Sometimes it is best not to plump for any one solution but to leave the final answer as a probability balanced among several possibilities. In any case, you should indicate how reliable you consider your reconstruction to be and suggest what further work would help to resolve outstanding uncertainties.

The preceding paragraphs should also help you come to grips with problems like number 9, in which you are asked to design a plan of research for the *Cuimayo basin* in order to generate the structured data and hypotheses that will make possible the drawing of valid inferences about patterns of zonal interaction in that Andean valley. As time and space are the dimensions of the contextual frame within which archaeological data are interpreted, the advice given is relevant in the other problems as well. Some of these are more narrowly focused, but the same principles are involved. Reference to an introductory text on method and theory for help on specific points, combined with some thought on your part, will supply any extra equipment needed to "solve" the problems. We are throwing you into the middle of the pool, not the deep end, and your toes can touch bottom.

Archaeology is a bit like a three-dimensional crossword puzzle with several clues missing, some answers in an unknown language, and a frame that changes as you move from one level to another. We enjoy it and hope that you do too.

The Island of Kufungua

Steve Daniels

The island of Kufungua lies in the Indian Ocean off the east coast of the Republic of Tumbia (fig. 1.1). The western part of the island is fertile and comparatively low-lying, rising gently from sea level to 250 meters. The rainfall here averages 900 mm a year and the vegetation is open savanna woodland. To the east the ground rises steeply and the whole of the eastern side of the island is mountainous. Rainfall in the rugged mountain terrain may reach 1600 mm a year, and the vegetation is mostly thick montane forest with occasional small patches of grassland.

At the present day there are two main tribes on Kufungua, the BaKata of the western lowlands and the BaHapa of the mountains. The languages of both peoples are classified as Bantu. That of the BaKata has a typically Bantu phonology and is very similar to the language of the BaLena who live on the coast of Tumbia opposite Kufungua. The language of the BaHapa, on the other hand, makes use of a click sound characteristic of the Khoisan family of languages spoken today by the Khoikhoi (Hottentots) and San (Bushmen) of southern Africa.

There is a reference to Kufungua in the log of João Carneira, a Portuguese captain whose ship, the Rose of Mateus, visited the island on Christmas Day, 1503:

> There is a good anchorage on the west coast of the Island of Kufungua where a sizable river runs down to the sea. The people of these parts, who are called the Kata, are prosperous and peaceful. They have large herds of cattle from which they obtain both meat and milk. They evidently did not fear that we would attack and made no warlike moves against us. With the aid of an interpreter, I learned that in olden days there had been much fighting on the island and that they had been often attacked by the Amabara, a fierce and barbarous people who lived high in the eastern mountains. The Kata were eventually victorious and the people of the mountains now no longer dared to attack them.

A team of archaeologists from the National University of Tumbia has been carrying out research on the mainland, in BaLena country, for the past 15 years. The later prehistoric sequence in this area is now blocked out and may be summarized as follows:

BACKGROUND INFORMATION

THE ARCHAEOLOGY OF TUMBIA

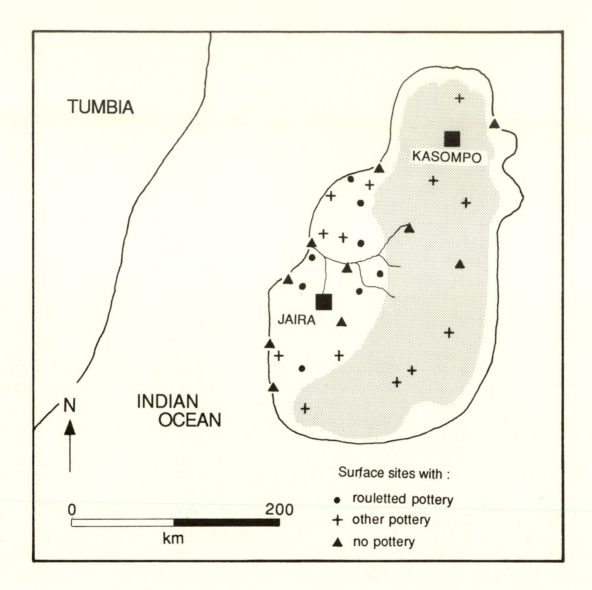

Figure 1.1. Archaeological sites on the island of Kufungua.

Later Stone Age: 12,000 B.C.—A.D. 300

The area was inhabited by hunter-gatherers whose physical type, as determined from skeletal remains, has been described as "Capoid," i.e., similar to that of the Khoikhoi and San. Small stone tools, including arrowheads, were made by flaking, and in the later part of the period ground stone axes were also manufactured. Rock shelters were used for temporary occupation and there were also open campsites. Along the coast, shell middens and bone fish-hooks show that there was considerable exploitation of coastal and maritime resources.

Early Iron Age: A.D. 300–1200

Immigrants of Negroid physical type appeared in the area at the beginning of this period. They cultivated millet, smelted and forged iron, and made pottery. At the beginning of the period, pottery was decorated almost entirely by stamping, but incision gradually became more popular and by the end of the period was used far more frequently. Cattle were kept and by A.D. 1200 were providing some 70% of the meat supply. The immigrants evidently intermarried with the Later Stone Age peoples, since many skeletons show both Negroid and Capoid features. Some elements of Later Stone Age culture also survived, for example ground stone axes which continued to be made as late as A.D. 1000. Comparison of the archaeological data with the linguistic evidence suggests that the immigrants were speakers of Bantu languages.

The beginning of the Later Iron Age is marked by the sudden appearance of a new technique of pottery decoration—rouletting. Rouletted designs were impressed on the pot by rolling an object, usually a twist of string or a small wooden cylinder, over its surface while the clay was still wet. This remained the dominant technique throughout the period. The economy continued basically the same as in the Early Iron Age, but the meat supply was now obtained almost entirely from domestic cattle. Skeletal remains of this period are fully Negroid, and it is generally considered that a new wave of Bantu-speaking immigrants was responsible for the innovations.

Later Iron Age: A.D. 1200–1700

Historical records, patchy at first but making reference to the BaLena, take up the story in the eighteenth century.

During the last five years the NUT has extended its interests from the mainland to Kufungua. There has been extensive reconnaissance work during which samples of 30 to 300 sherds have been collected from a number of sites. Two test excavations have been made, and the tables and notes below present a summary of the more important data recovered.

ARCHAEOLOGICAL WORK IN KUFUNGUA

1. Jaira Mound

LEVEL	DECORATIVE TECHNIQUES ON POTTERY (%)				RADIOCARBON DATES
	STAMPED	INCISED	ROULETTED	OTHER	
1	1	12	68	19	
2	4	10	74	12	1560–1660 cal. A.D.
3	3	9	70	18	1360–1500 cal. A.D.
4	67	16	—	17	
5	66	11	—	23	
6	64	17	—	19	
7	67	13	—	20	
8	—	—	—	—	170 cal. B.C.–70 cal. A.D.

No pottery was found in level 8, which contained numerous flaked stone tools and a number of ground stone axes. In levels 1 to 7 the only stone tools were three ground stone axes from level 7 and one from level 6.

Level 3 yielded a sherd of glazed Black-on-Yellow Islamic ware, known to have been manufactured in Southern Arabia in the early fourteenth century. Iron slag and occasional tools including hoes and spearheads were found throughout Levels 1–7.

A preliminary analysis of the fauna from the site showed that the bones from level 8 were all of wild animals. This level also produced fish remains and a few pieces of turtle shell. In level 7 about 30% of the bones were of domestic cattle, and this proportion increased to 56% in level 4. In levels 1 to 3 domestic cattle accounted for over 90% of the animal bones.

Several human skeletons were recovered. Four from Level 6 exhibited mixtures of Capoid and Negroid characteristics. A single skeleton from level 3 was typically Negroid.

2. Kasompo Cave

LEVEL	DECORATIVE TECHNIQUES ON POTTERY (%)				RADIOCARBON DATES
	STAMPED	INCISED	ROULETTED	OTHER	
1	58	15	1	26	1635–1715 cal. A.D.
2	53	11	—	36	1330–1450 cal. A.D.
3	—	—	—	—	1340–1500 cal. A.D.
4	—	—	—	—	7300–6900 cal. B.C.

Levels 3 and 4 produced abundant flaked stone tools together with bones of antelope and wild pig but no potsherds. In levels 1 and 2 most of the animal bones were of wild species, but some 25% were of domestic cattle.

A human skeleton from level 3 was of Capoid type. Level 1 yielded an iron hoe, while level 2 contained two iron hoes, a ground stone ax and several small flaked stone arrowheads.

Dr. Kwaheri of the NUT Archaeology Department is preparing a grant application for further work on Kufungua and has asked you to contribute a summary reconstruction of Kufungua prehistory based on the evidence presently available. He tells you that the assessors are likely to be especially interested in the correlation of the island and mainland sequences and in the question of the changing relationships among race, language, and culture on the island.

ADDENDUM   In preparing your solution to this and similar problems you will find it useful to set out the data in tabular form. Figure 1.2 is an (intentionally incomplete) example of such a table. Summarizing in this way the data that are most critical for the definition of cultural continuities and changes makes it relatively easy to assign assemblages to phases and cultures. Next you will wish to incorporate other data, for example the evidence of surface sites, into the picture you are building up of cultural variation across time and space. What you are doing is often known by the grand name of time-space systematics. When you have developed a table that specifies, demarcates, and categorizes cultural variation in the area and periods under consideration, you still must recognize that data organization does not in itself constitute problem resolution. For that you need to infer and document the processes, not necessarily only cultural, that have generated the patterning displayed by the data.

It is here that your imagination, informed by all you have ever experienced directly or indirectly of the world in general and of human behavior in particular, comes into play to suggest analogues that might have produced the materials you are studying. Your interpretations will also be influenced and guided by your theory or theories of human behavior (rarely made explicit) and

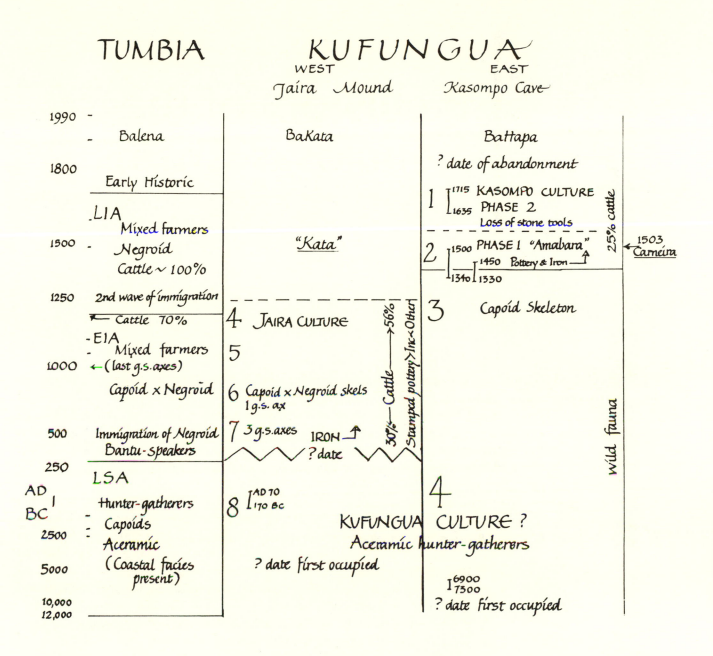

Figure 1.2. Partial tabulation of Kufungua data.

by those of the natural sciences. Within that frame the principal constraint on inference is a continual working backwards and forwards between data and intuitively derived ideas, a procedure that may be formalized as the testing of hypotheses. Ultimately you should be able to superimpose the cultural processes (diffusion, militarization, economic intensification, intermarriage, etc., etc.) on the table, as a sort of and perhaps as an actual overlay. An explanatory commentary that sets out your conclusions and the arguments in their support is all that is needed to complete an answer—one that hopefully will not superfluously repeat information given as part of the problem itself, nor force the reader to follow all the tortuous and dead-end lines of reasoning that you, like everyone else, go through to achieve your results.

N.D. & J.D.

Prehistory of the Nebulosas Chain

BACKGROUND

The Nebulosas are islands formed by volcanos that burst through a limestone plateau that is today submerged beneath 40 fathoms of ocean. The island chain extends from the Digitus Peninsula of Illysium to the western shore of Obscurata (fig. 2.1). Relations between these two nations have long been strained by a frontier dispute. In part for this reason, but also because of great differences in language, the flow of archaeological information between the two powers is no more than a trickle.

The climate is oceanic and temperate, due to a warm ocean current that wells up along the southern reaches of the chain. Its meeting and intermingling with an Arctic countercurrent produces the dense fogs for which the islands are named, but also an incredibly rich and diverse marine life that compensates for the absence of a terrestrial mammalian macrofauna.

Today the islands are largely deserted save for a few weather stations and scattered military outposts. The former Lert population was almost exterminated by diseases brought by European sailors in the late seventeenth century; the few survivors have been relocated to mainland areas.

According to a brief account written by a supercargo on the galleon Icarus which had put in to Helios Island for careening in 1658, the native people there were friendly to the point of inviting him to stay and be a Lert. Their village of semi-subterranean dwellings was located on the seashore just above the reach of the equinoctial spring tides. He describes them as expert seafarers possessing skin-covered boats of amazing speed and stability. From these, using skillfully made harpoons of bone with inset stone tips, they hunted sea mammals, "fearing not to assail Leviathan upon the watery deep."

ARCHAEOLOGICAL DATA

While the evidence from Obscurata is very scanty indeed, rumors have reached Illysium of the finding of a site on Ignota island with a prismatic core technology capable of producing long blades. No date has been suggested.

Archaeological investigation of the Nebulosas has recently been promoted by the Illysory government in an effort to strengthen its claim over the island chain by demonstrating that the Lerts had originally settled the area from their mainland rather than, as argued by Obscuratist scholars, from the

Figure 2.1. The Nebulosas island chain and adjacent mainlands. Prehistoric sites are indicated.

east. Numerous sites have been located and four excavated: Foggy Bottom on Drygalski Island, the Echinus Bay site on Helios, Hecate Beach on nearby Erebus, and the mainland site of Lingula Inlet (figs. 2.1 and 2.2). A brief description of the sites and finds follows (fig. 2.3 and table 2.1).

Foggy Bottom, Drygalski Island

This village site, located a little inland, has given a single occupation level dated at 9500 ± 350 B.P. Among the artifacts found were many of obsidian and chert, including large blades and microblades and numerous bifacially worked artifacts such as points, scrapers, and end-set points, the latter occasionally made of greenstone. Faunal remains were sparse but included clams, periwinkle shells, an occasional seal bone, and a few sea urchin shells.

Echinus Bay, Helios Island

The site is located well above the current tide line near a stream flowing into Echinus Bay. A limited excavation revealed the existence of a succession of settlements and their adjacent middens.

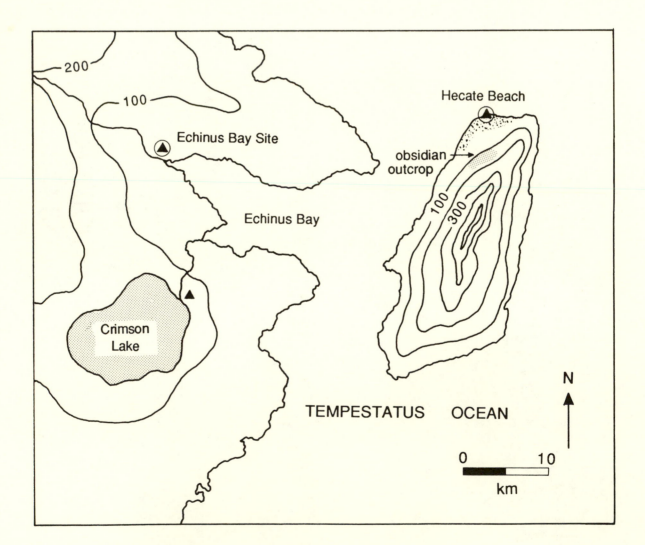

Figure 2.2. Prehistoric sites on Helios and Erebus Islands.

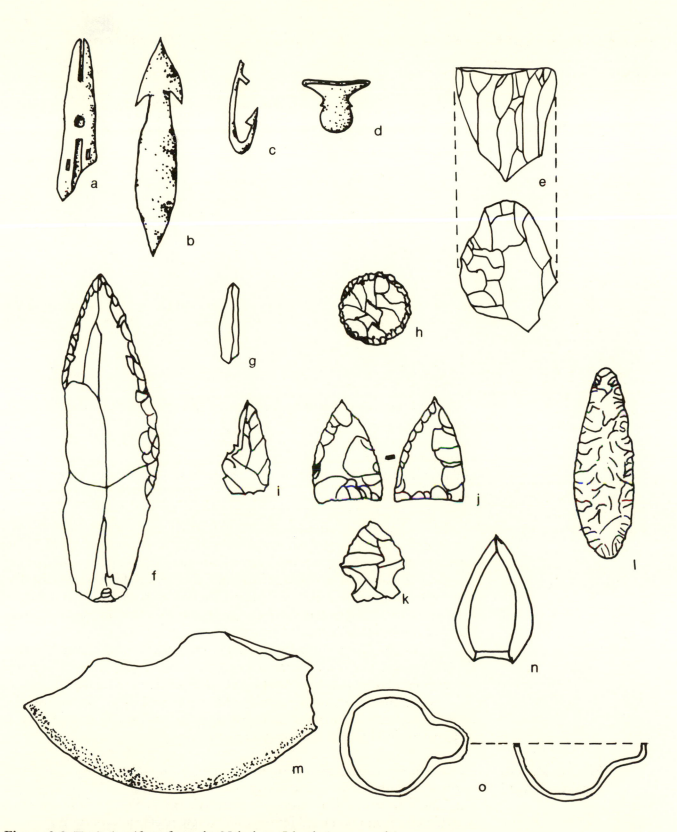

Figure 2.3. Typical artifacts from the Nebulosas Islands (not to scale).
Bone and ivory: (a) toggling harpoon head with end slot; (b) barbed harpoon head; (c) hook; (d) labret.
Obsidian and chert: (e) prismatic core; (f) large blade; (g) microblade; (h) bifacial discoid scraper; (i) bifacial burin; (j) bifacial end-set point; (k) bifacial point; (l) bifacial knife.
Ground slate: (m) knife; (n) end-set harpoon point.
Igneous rock: (o) pecked lamp.

TABLE 2.1 Percentage Frequencies of Selected Artifact Types and ^{14}C Dates by Site and Level.

SITES	ARTIFACTS					^{14}C DATES B.P.*
	BLADES	(FLAKED) BIFACIALS	GROUND SLATE	BONE & IVORY	MISC. & OTHER	
Foggy Btm	20	60	—	10	10	9500 ± 350
Echinus Bay						
Level 1	—	—	50	40	10	
Level 2	—	40	—	55	5	
Level 3	20	30	—	40	10	8000 ± 300
Hecate Bch	85	—	2	8	5	
Lingula Inlet						
Level 1	—	5	65	25	5	
Level 2	—	25	50	20	5	1500 ± 100

* Laboratory numbers not supplied.

Level 1 represents the latest occupation. The site at this and the preceding stage was extensive and can fairly be called a village of pithouses. Among the materials recovered were ground slate objects including knives and harpoon point insets known as endblades. Ivory and bone toggling harpoon heads with slotted ends were present, as were pecked stone lamps and labrets. Faunal material included quantities of seal, some whale and sea otter, remains of pelagic fish species and salmon, and clam and sea urchin shells.

Levels 1 and 2 are separated by a thin horizon of distinctive volcanic ash, the product of an eruption, firmly dated to 3870 ± 40 B.P., that formed the crater now filled by Crimson Lake, named after an extraordinary algal bloom.

Level 2 contained no ground slate artifacts; bifacially worked obsidian tools were common, and included burins. Barbed harpoon heads of bone and ivory were of non-toggling types. Associated faunal remains included sea lions, many sea otters, clam shells, and an occasional whale bone.

Level 3 represents a smaller settlement than the above. Flaked obsidian artifacts included bifacially worked points, scrapers, and knives, occurring together with bone and ivory hooks and shell pendants. The faunal remains consisted mostly of sea urchin shells, with clams and other littoral fish and shellfish forming the remainder. Bones of sea lion were present, though rare, in the upper portion of the associated midden.

Hecate Beach, Erebus Island

About 50 artifacts have been recovered eroding from a low cliff associated with a storm beach that is still occasionally swept by high tides. The site has given long, finely made obsidian blades and prismatic cores. There was no evidence of architecture, and no faunal remains save a few reindeer/caribou bones.

Lingula Inlet Site, Illysium

At this site two phases of occupation were tentatively identified on the basis of the overlapping outlines of pit houses. This observation was later confirmed in the lab when it was shown that there were discontinuities in the vertical distribution of ground slate tools and bifacially worked artifacts. The former occur in especially high frequencies in the upper level (1). In addition, it was noted that while whale bone was absent in level 2, it was common in level 1 together with remains of other deep sea species.

Harpoon head styles also underwent a shift from a toggling type in level 1 to a non-toggling form with rudimentary barbs in level 2. Caribou bone was sparsely represented in both levels, while fish remains, particularly salmon, were common in level 2.

Use the data supplied to construct a summary table of the prehistory of the Nebulosas. What can be said of the subsistence practices of the prehistoric phases/cultures identified and of their relation to changes in technology and tool kits? Lastly, how strong is the Illysory case for a Lert penetration of the island chain from the west?

PROBLEM 3

The Repton Barrow

Pamela Bowyer

RECENT EXCAVATIONS

The Repton Long Barrow is situated between the parish church and the River Esk in Repton, Bluffshire, U.K. (fig. 3.1). You spent part of last summer examining evidence for previous disturbance of the site, with a view to assessing the extent to which the original Neolithic burial mound remained intact. You excavated a depression at the east end of the site, and found that it cut through the original Neolithic mound, and was filled with a mixture of chalk rubble, flint nodules, topsoil, Victorian refuse, a halfpenny dated 1814, and a plaque inscribed "Open'd 1819 P.B-H." Removing the fill of the trench made it possible to clean and draw the western section (stratigraphic profile), in which layers of the barrow could be seen clearly (fig. 3.2). You have also cleaned and drawn the western section of the road cut through the western end of the barrow (fig. 3.3).

While cleaning the sections you recovered a number of artifacts and human bones. These are described in Table 3.1, and their stratigraphic position is marked on Figures 3.2 and 3.3. The strata identified during section drawing are listed in Table 3.2.

To assist in interpreting the history of the barrow you have gathered all documentary sources pertaining to the site. These are reproduced in the following sections.

HISTORICAL DOCUMENTS

The following letter was translated from the Latin by Robert Stubbs in his *Life of St. Vincent,* London, 1845:

> Brother Wilfrid, of the Abbey Church of St. Vincent, humble servant of the servants of the Blessed Mother of God, to his most dear brothers and fellow servants. Great is the work of the Lord, excellent in all of His will. The pious inhabitants of Rypptowne have combined to aid in the construction of their church by transporting the material, making pathways, and hauling the wagons, all that is necessary for the great work. Our Lord has rewarded their humble zeal by miracles. In the path of a newly made road, we were led to discover the resting place of our patron saint. The monks, full of praise and exultation, opened the tomb of St. Vincent and extricated him from the earth, in his sepulchre of marble, wondrously carved, with scenes from the life of Our Lord, and the inscription VINCENZO VIVATIS IN CHRISTO. They disposed him under the site of the altar of the Holy Cross of the nave, the stones for which were collected and brought also from his burial place. The people of our land, therefore, having received divine blessing, great miracles are frequently wrought in our church. Given in this year of the Incarnate Word, one thousand one hundred thirty six. Farewell.

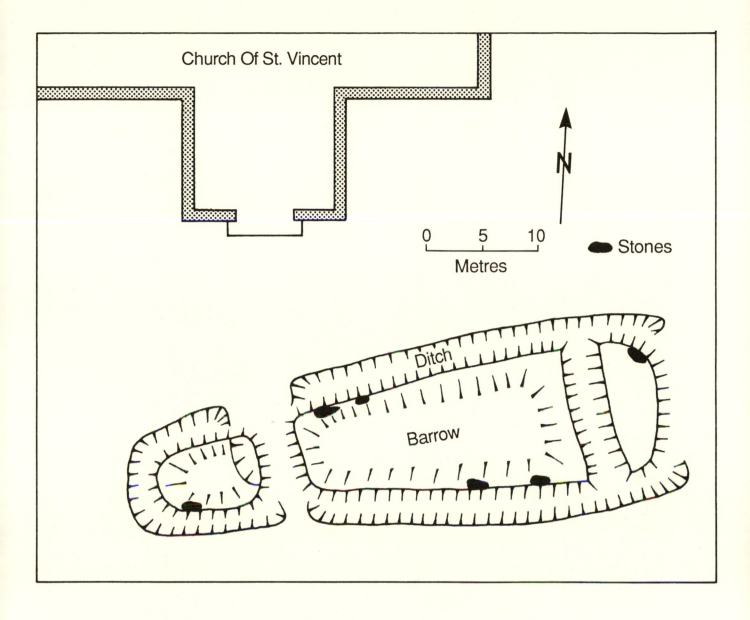

Figure 3.1. The Repton Long Barrow.

The next document is an excerpt from the field notes of the antiquarian Reverend William Hartley (1715–1767):

> On September 9, 1744, we undertook to excavate the large Priestess's Barrow near Ripton-on-Esk. In this tumulus, we found the Skeleton of a Female, posited on its back. Mix'd with the Bones, very much decay'd, were bits of a bronze Metal, among them a mirror, also broken clay, and a glass Chalice. We gather'd also an Ornament which, I flatter myself, is altogether one of the most Curious, and for its size, Costly pieces of Antiquity ever discover'd. It lay near the Neck, or, rather, more toward the right shoulder of the Priestess; it is entirely of Gold, and is most elegantly and richly set with Garnets.

Note: The artifacts entered Reverend Hartley's private collection, and can today be seen in the Museum of the Bluffshire County Archaeological Society, together with illustrations from Hartley's notebooks (fig. 3.4).

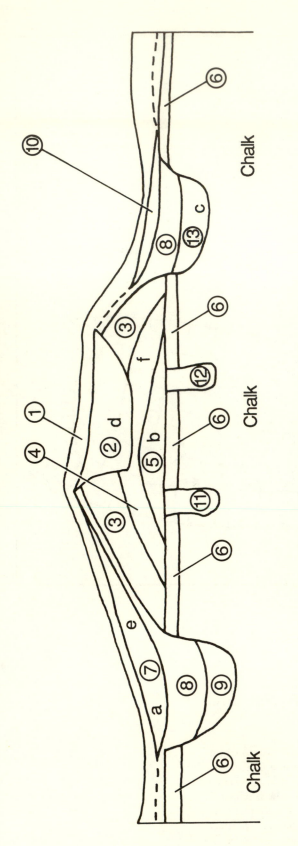

Figure 3.2. Layers observed in the west wall of old trench through eastern end of barrow.

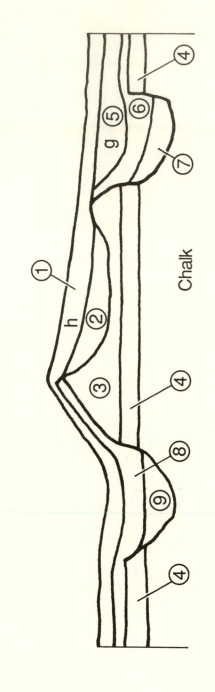

Figure 3.3. Layers observed in the west wall of old road cut through western end of barrow.

TABLE 3.1   Artifacts Found During Section Cleaning. Position of the Artifacts is Indicated on Figures 3.2 and 3.3.

A. Objects Found in Western Section of Eastern Trench.

a. Fragment of bronze, highly polished on one side, inscribed "Avgvsta"
b. Human femur
c. Antler pick
d. Penny dated 1739
e. Fragment of glass
f. Broken ground stone axe

B. Objects Found in Western Section of Western Road Cut

g. Silver coin of Constantine the Great (288–337 A.D.)
h. 18 sherds of early Medieval pottery (c. 1200 A.D.)

TABLE 3.2   Description of Strata Recorded on Figures 3.2 and 3.3.

A. Strata on Figure 3.2

1. Modern topsoil
2. Mixture of topsoil, chalk rubble, and flint nodules
3. Sterile chalk rubble and flint nodules
4. Pile of turves
5. Earthen mound
6. Buried soil
7. Chalk rubble and flint nodules
8. Topsoil, undistinguishable from layer 1, except where separated by layers 7 and 10.
9. Silt, with occasional chalk fragments
10. Same as 7
11. Black soil with wood fragments
12. Same as 11
13. Same as 9

B. Strata on Figure 3.3

1. Modern topsoil
2. Topsoil and chalk fragments
3. Sterile chalk rubble and flint nodules
4. Buried soil
5. Chalk rubble and topsoil
6. Soil
7. Silt
8. Soil
9. Silt

The following excerpts are from *Ancient Bluffshire*, 1830, by Peter Burke-Holt (1793–1835), one of Britain's first field archaeologists.

[p.iv] We have evidence of the very high antiquity of these sepulchral memorials, but none regarding the tribes to whom they appertained, that can rest on a solid foundation. I have no doubt but that the greater part of our Bluffshire barrows were the sepulchral monuments of the Celtic and first colonists of Britain.

[p.46] In the excavation of a broad barrow near St. Vincent's in Repton, we dug a trench across the east end and, upon nearing the midpoint, came upon a pile of bones lying in a confused and irregular manner, all thrown promiscuously together. They had been well preserved from their long deposition deep in the chalk, as they would bear being thrown a considerable distance without breaking. The position of the bones at the centre of the barrow and upon the natural earth evidently proves them to have been a primary deposit. On either side of the bones were a number of round cists dug into the native earth and filled with charred wood. Over all the area in the centre of the barrow was a pyramid of loose flints and turves. We are obliged to confess our ignorance for what meaning these cists and layers might have.

The Ornament

The Glass Chalice

Sketches from the notebook of Reverend Hartley

Figure 3.4. Sketches from the Reverend William Hartley's notebooks, Bluffshire County Archaeological Society archives.

From *A Catalogue of Anglo-Saxon Jewellery* by A. Outbridge-Brown, chapter 4, "Disc Brooches":

> No. 473 (Cat. MBCAS, Hartley Coll. 2342). Finely worked circular gold disc (type 3a), inlaid with garnet and cloissonné enamel. Probably late fifth century on stylistic grounds. Ref. *A Bluffshire Antiquarian,* R. P. Hartley, Dalesman Books, 1958.

From *Trade in Saxon England* by N. P. Johnson, Society for British Archaeology, 1978:

> Saxon glasswork appears to have been traded largely from the continent in the period 450 to 600 A.D. Much of the glass has been recovered from cemeteries, and includes particularly fine examples of Rhenish claw-beakers, such as those found in East Anglia and in the Repton "Priestess" barrow.

From *A Glossary of Prehistoric England* by G. Creuse, 1984:

> Long barrows: oval or trapezoidal burial mounds associated with Early Neolithic (q.v.). Constructed of earth, turf, or rubble. Quarry ditches usually on either side. Available evidence (antler picks, cattle scapula shovels) suggests that construction was undertaken with fairly simple tools, presumably employed by large numbers of people. Skeletons range from one to dozens, usually buried under a mortuary structure, generally at the higher and thicker end. Associated artifacts rare, but may include pottery and ground stone axes.

As a keen student of M.B. Schiffer's *Behavioral Archaeology* (New York: Academic Press, 1976), you are aware that artifacts may be found in primary or secondary contexts, and that a variety of cultural and natural processes are involved in the deposition and burial of artifacts. Can you account for the artifacts recovered from the Repton Barrow and for the configuration of features and layers recorded in your section drawings?

PROBLEM 4

Entre-Deux-Lacs

SETTING   The Entre-Deux-Lacs area is a narrow stretch of land lying between two large lakes in Eastern North America (fig. 4.1). The area encompasses two ecological zones. To the north of Lake Nakawa, bedrock consists of hard, glacially scoured pre-Cambrian rocks which support a thin soil unsuitable for agriculture. The natural vegetation is a mixed coniferous/hardwood forest. The modern economy is based on mining, logging, and tourism. To the south of Lake Nakawa, bedrock is limestone, overlain by glacial till and outwash sands and gravels in the valleys. Mixed farming, the wine industry, and market gardening have largely removed the original cover of hardwood forest. Aboriginal varieties of corn could be grown as far north as Lake Nakawa, but tobacco could be grown north of Sturgeon River only in exceptionally good years.

A pollen core from Fish Lake shows that the types of vegetation seen in the region today were established by 2000 B.C. Forest clearance (presumably resulting from agriculture) began by 1150 A.D. and intensified between 1350 and 1550. From 1650 to 1800 there was some regeneration; the final clearance took place throughout the nineteenth century.

HISTORY   The area was described briefly by two Europeans in the seventeenth century. Santerre, under orders from the French crown, explored the region in 1625:

> Passing north of a large lake, which we named Lac des Iles, we traveled through a barren land with many lakes and marshes surrounded by deep forest. We met no Indians, although our guide pointed to signs of their camps. The area would be worthless were it not for the abundance of beaver. Traveling on west of Lac des Iles, we descended to a wooded land in which were many fields of corn. These Indians live in long huts made of the boughs of trees and thatched with bark. These are defended by flimsy stockades, yet no violence was offered to us. At our approach they proffered corn for our tobacco. We asked about furs, and they assured us that they could obtain them from the north if we left tobacco with them. We resolved to travel further to the northwest, in search of furs.

Courtemanche set up a Jesuit mission at Fish Lake. Shortly before it was abandoned in 1636 due to increasing hostility from local Indians, Courtemanche wrote in his journal:

> The Indians delight in fighting and we fear for the safety of our brethren. The warriors leave the work of tending the fields to the women (except that they jealously hoe their small gardens of tobacco) and delight to smoke and plan war. We encourage them to obtain furs, for by trade their minds might be diverted from fighting. They covet our axes (which we offer in exchange for furs), but say that furs can be obtained only by fighting their enemies to the north.

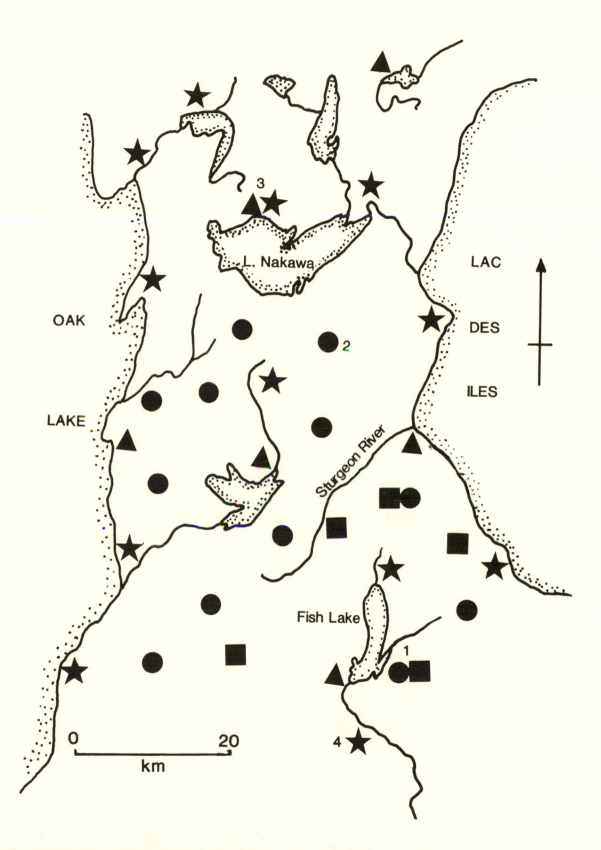

Figure 4.1. Location of archaeological sites in the Entre-Deux-Lacs region. Triangle: chipped stone assemblage with spear points. Star: chipped stone assemblages with side-notched arrowheads. Circle: longhouse villages with sand-tempered pottery. Square: longhouse villages with shell-tempered pottery.

ARCHAEOLOGY   Sites found during archaeological survey are shown in Figure 4.1. Four sites have been excavated in the region.

Site 1   This site was extensively excavated, and three superimposed villages of long-houses were found. Ploughing had disturbed the topsoil and removed all trace of house floors. Postmolds survived in the undisturbed soil below, and careful mapping revealed the shapes of longhouses and their sequence of construction. Associated with longhouses were pits which produced the only artifacts which could be related to the cultural sequence. The excavator defined three periods of use for the site.

In *Period I* there was a small village of 3 longhouses, each about 25 m long. The following artifacts were found. Chipped stone: side-notched arrow points, scrapers, drills, awls, knives; sand-tempered pottery with cord impressions; bone tools: scapula hoe, awls, needles, fish-hooks; ground stone: polished axes from pre-Cambrian rocks, pipes from stone only obtainable to the south of the region. The pottery was typologically similar to pottery found to the south of the region, and the pipes were identical to those found to the south. The fauna was mainly deer and fish, although a wide range of other species were also found in small numbers. The flora included large quantities of hickory nuts, acorns, and chenopods. A small amount of corn was also found. A radiocarbon date of 1190 to 1250 cal. A.D. was obtained.

In *Period II* the village had grown to 10 rectangular houses, each about 40 m long. The village was defended by a palisade. Artifacts were similar to those in Period I, but much of the pottery was decorated with a punctate design, unlike any style known outside the region. Fauna and flora were the same, with the addition of tobacco seeds, and corn cobs were more common than in the previous period. Radiocarbon dates of 1280 to 1350 cal. A.D. and 1320 to 1410 cal. A.D. were obtained.

The *Period III* village was built partially over the Period II village which appears to have been burnt. Five ovoid longhouses are present, each about 40 m long. Artifacts were similar to those of Periods I and II, with the following changes: arrowheads were corner-notched; pottery was shell-tempered with incised decoration identical to that from fifteenth-century sites to the southeast; ground stone axes were made of local chert; stone pipes were plentiful.

Site 2   Test excavations revealed the corner of a longhouse and part of a palisade. Pottery was exclusively sand-tempered, and included cord and punctate designs. Large numbers of ground stone axes made of pre-Cambrian rock were found. Stone and pottery pipes were present. No record of fauna and flora is available. A radiocarbon date of 1400 to 1450 cal. A.D. was obtained on a palisade post.

Site 3   This site lies on the northern shore of Lake Nakawa in a sheltered bay. Deposits consist of cultural layers interspersed with beach sand.

Occupation 1, the lowest layer, contained spear points, bifacial knives, scrapers and drills of local chert, roughly flaked axes with polished ends made from pre-Cambrian metamorphic rock, and bone tools such as awls, fish-hooks, and pins. Faunal material included abundant fish remains and some deer, as well as occasional specimens of northern furbearers. A radiocarbon date of 1520 to 1410 cal. B.C. was obtained on charcoal from a hearth.

Occupation 2, with a radiocarbon date of 180 to 270 cal. A.D., contained side-notched arrowheads, a range of chipped stone tools similar to those of Occupation 1, and ground and polished axes of pre-Cambrian rock. Fauna was the same as for Occupation 1.

Occupation 3 is undated. It contained the same assemblage as Occupation 2, with the addition of two sherds of cord-impressed sand-tempered pottery. Stone pipes identical to those in Sites 1 and 2 appeared.

Occupation 4, with a date of 1240 to 1350 cal. A.D., also contained an assemblage similar to that of Occupation 2. Ground and polished axes were more common. A few sherds of punctate pottery were found, as well as three carbonized corn kernels and a corn cob. Fauna was similar to that for Occupation 2, with a higher frequency of furbearers.

Occupation 5 contains an assemblage identical to that of Occupation 4, except that stone pipes were replaced by sand-tempered pottery pipes with very small bowls.

In *Occupation 6* there were only historic (post-1700 A.D.) artifacts. Fauna was dominated by furbearers and fish.

Site 4

This site, which lies to the south of Fish Lake, was tested briefly and found to consist of a freshwater shell midden containing numerous fish and deer bones. Artifacts of chipped chert included side-notched arrow points. Ground stone artifacts included edge-ground roughly flaked axes of pre-Cambrian rocks and local chert, but no pipes were recovered. Bone tools included fish-hooks, awls, and pins.

On the basis of the information given above, reconstruct the prehistory of the Entre-Deux-Lacs area. Pay attention to changes in prehistoric economy and their causes.

PROBLEM 5

The Neolithic of Arak

Curtis Runnels

Soon after taking a position as assistant professor of Near Eastern archaeology at the state university, you receive the following letter:

INTERNATIONAL LIGHTWEIGHT RESEARCH FOUNDATION
15 L'Enfant Plaza
Washington, D.C.

Mon., 4 Jan. 19––

Dear Colleague:

Professor Rhys Pelaf's archaeological expedition was forced recently to terminate its important excavation of the neolithic site of Tell Al-Felafel in the country of Arak, near the capital of Taboule, because of deteriorating political conditions and indigestion. Before the end of the excavation, the archaeologists were confident they had discovered an important site showing evidence of surprising social and economic complexity. The site is located on the Arakian dry upland, and even today this area is good for farming and herding. The site is far, however, from sources of exotic raw materials such as Persian Gulf shells, Sinai turquoise, lapis lazuli (an azure blue semiprecious stone) from Afghanistan, and Turkish obsidian (fig. 5.1). Professor Pelaf and his assistant, the Arakian archaeologist Dr. Olive Tahini, were able to clear only part of the site, revealing stone foundations of a massive wall and a number of buildings. After clearing enough fill to expose the plans of the buildings (fig. 5.2), they had time only to dig three rooms in building A, one room each in buildings D and E, and most of the small building J (fig. 5.3). To the southeast of the site a cemetery was discovered and partly excavated by Professor Pelaf's other assistant, Dr. Rich Humus (fig. 5.4). Some of the graves were provided with abundant grave goods (e.g., fig. 5.5).

Unfortunately, Professor Pelaf and the other expedition archaeologists, after their experience in Arak, have decided to go into other professions and have left their rough field notes and sketches unstudied and unpublished. The Foundation supported this expedition and needs an assessment of the data in order to determine whether additional work would be desirable. Members of the Foundation are afraid to go to Arak themselves, and, frankly, we don't know what to do next, except to write you this letter. Knowing your expertise in this area, the Foundation would be grateful if you would analyze the Pelaf expedition field notes and sketches and submit a report at your earliest convenience.

The important question for the Foundation is this: evidence from other sites indicates that soon after the appearance of agriculture, settlements began to increase in size and complexity (much like the Foundation!). Why did this happen? Do the Tell Al-Felafel data suggest any connection between agriculture, or anything else for that matter, and increasing cultural complexity? The Foundation is only interested in the broad outlines, since we are worried that we might have to pay to dig lots of sites up. We want your observations and generalizations based on the limited data we have enclosed. I suspect that the Trustees will vote you the usual minuscule fee upon receipt of your report. Do keep this brief; their attention span has been somewhat abbreviated by *anno domini*.

With our thanks in advance for your assistance, I remain,
Sincerely,

Ethelbert Milquetoast
Bureaucrat

Enclosures: Pelaf Expedition field notes and drawings.

PROFESSOR RHYS PELAF'S FIELD NOTES (SLIGHTLY EDITED BY E.M).
DAY BOOK OF THE EXCAVATIONS IN THE ROOMS (FIGS. 5.2 AND 5.3).

Building A, Room 1. Began clearing possible shrine today. Three female figurines, one in a soft stone (see fig. 5.3) on a low clay platform at one end of room. One resembles figurine found by Humus yesterday in cemetery? Two

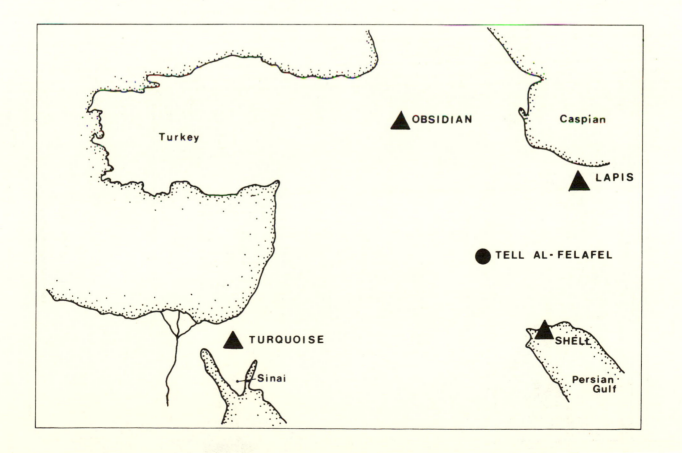

Figure 5.1. Map showing the location of Tell Al-Felafel and of sources of exotic materials.

Figure 5.2. Plan of Tell Al-Felafel (insets are at 2x overall scale).

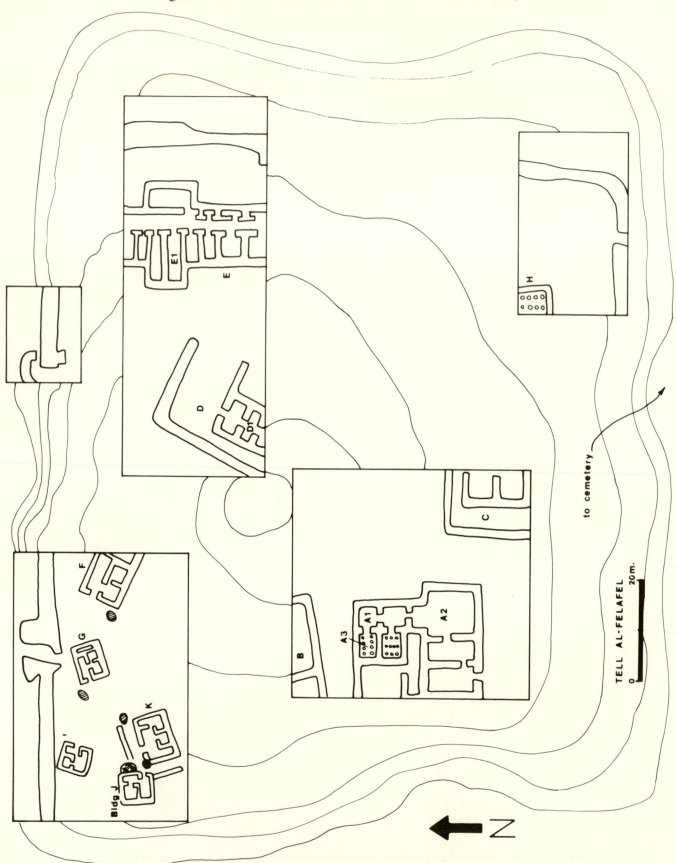

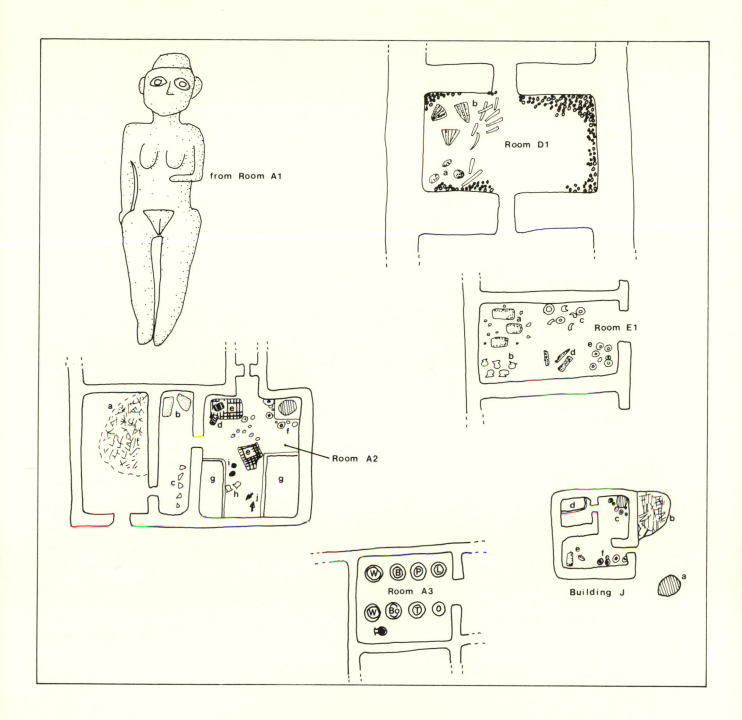

Figure 5.3. Page from Professor Pelaf's notebook.

small piles of carbonized barley in a pottery dish on the same small clay platform as the figurines. Horn cores from domesticated goats fallen from a small clay wall niche to one side. Several painted pots contain both sheep and goat bones (burned). Two quartz crystals were found in one corner of the room. Flecks of carbon noticeable throughout the collapsed mudbrick fill.

Building A, Room 2. My assistant Tahini is excavating a possible domestic area adjacent to the "shrine." She reports that outside the door to the west is a pile of burned bones, sherds, obsidian chips, and miscellaneous debris (a). The bones belong to sheep, goats, cows, and pigs. There is a small number of wild animal bones as well. Inside the first room, two millstones (b) and 5 spindle whorls or weights (c). Inside main room, two carbonized wooden boxes (d), traces of carbonized woolen cloths (e), a raised and ash-filled fireplace with sherds of painted and coarse pots nearby (f), two raised clay benches or platforms (g), two marine shells (h), two obsidian mirrors (i), and two obsidian arrowheads or spearheads (j). Many flecks of carbon here, too. This room, and perhaps all of building A, destroyed by fire? There were many chips of obsidian and burned bones scattered throughout the fill.

Building A, Room 3. I am clearing small side room today. Eight large coarse clay jars (up to 1.5 m in height) found lined up in rows. Two contained wheat; 1 had barley; 1 peas; and 1 lentils. All the plant parts were carbonized. One pot was empty; 1 contained 450 bone beads; and 1 jar had 45 kg of unworked turquoise lumps. A small worked stone (an amulet, or seal?) with incised spiral decoration found on floor.

Building D, Room 1. Not feeling very well today. Have moved to large complex of structures in NE part of site. Three rounded cobblestones (perhaps with use wear from hammering) along with 10 good blades of obsidian, and three obsidian blade cores were noted. Hundreds of chips and small flakes of obsidian were collected, and many had been pushed to one side of the room.

Building E, Room 1. Feeling worse today. Continue in NE sector. Building E is only foundation with many small windowless rooms and only one narrow entrance. Three millstones with many small flakes of marine shell found in one corner of a typical small room (a). Also in the room were 5 whole marine shells (b), a pile of marine shell pieces and broken arm rings (c), three sandstone fragments (d), and 7 complete marine shell arm rings (e).

Building J. I am rushing to complete the excavation. Tahini and Humus are already too ill to go on. An empty, clay-lined pit was found in front of this building (a). A bone pile with sheep, goat, pig, and many wild animal bones, plus many coarse sherds, flint flakes, and other debris, found by the front door (b). Inside this poorly-constructed building were three rooms: one had 5 coarse pottery jars (f) and 2 millstones (e). Another room has an ash-filled pit in the floor (c) and 6 coarse pottery jars. the last room contained only a poorly built low clay platform (d).

(At this point the notes break off with the words "I don't feel very well-constructed myself . . ."—E.M.)

*   *   *

FROM DR. RICH HUMUS'S NOTES:
THE CEMETERY (FIG. 5.4)

Only part of the cemetery could be excavated. Surface depressions and sherd scatters indicated that more than 190 graves remain to be excavated.

All graves are sunk into the soft chalky rock of a river bluff about 200 m southeast of Tell Al-Felafel. The burials were numbered as they were discovered, and the sex and approximate age determinations were made by me on the spot using the preserved skeletal material. The following is a preliminary catalogue for each grave.

1. Male, 30 years, Spearhead of obsidian found lodged in chest cavity. Bones of previous burial pushed to side when this burial made. Grave goods: 10 obsidian spearheads; 10 obsidian dagger blades; 1 flint dagger with ivory handle carved to represent a snake; 5 obsidian mirrors; 6 painted jars containing carbonized wheat, barley, and peas; 21 lumps of unworked turquoise or lapis lazuli; and 1 large obsidian core.

2. Male (?), mid 20s. No grave offerings.

3. Infant, 2 years. No offerings.

4. Female, early 20s. Two coarse pottery jars, unpainted. One broken in half.

5. Male, 40 years. Offerings include: 7 bone beads; 4 obsidian mirrors; 5 painted pots; 15 obsidian dagger blades; more than 10 obsidian spearheads (not all were removed before the end of the excavation).

6. Female, mid-teens. Offerings include: 2 obsidian mirrors; 3 sea shell arm rings; 4 spindle whorls; 1 sea shell filled with red coloring matter.

7. Female, mid-teens. Unhealed cut marks on front of neck vertebrae. Offerings include: 2 obsidian mirrors; 2 sea shell ornaments (broken pieces only); 1 spindle whorl.

8. Male, mid-20s. This is the richest grave (fig. 5.5). Pit is carefully cut into the rock. Traces of a decayed wooden sarcophagus were noted by the excavation foreman, Mr. Babaganouj. Healed cuts on left upper arm bone (fig. 5.5:s); unhealed puncture wound at right of breast bone (t). Offerings include: headdress of lapis lazuli beads (a); 2 obsidian mirrors (b); necklace of bone beads (c); 2 fine painted jars (d); a pile of human bones from at least two previous burials (e); two shell arm rings (f, i); many little squares of cut and perforated lapis (g); 8 obsidian spearheads (h); a dagger with ivory handle in the form of an animal and with a fine flint blade (j); a soft stone female figurine (k); a lapis lazuli ring (l); 5 obsidian dagger blades (m); 19 bone beads (n); 9 obsidian blades (o); 3 large painted pottery jars (p); 10 lumps of unworked turquoise (q); and 3 marine shells (r).

9. Male (?) child, about 5 years. Grave offerings include: 1 stone female figurine; 1 obsidian dagger with bone handle; 2 obsidian spearheads; 2 lapis lazuli beads.

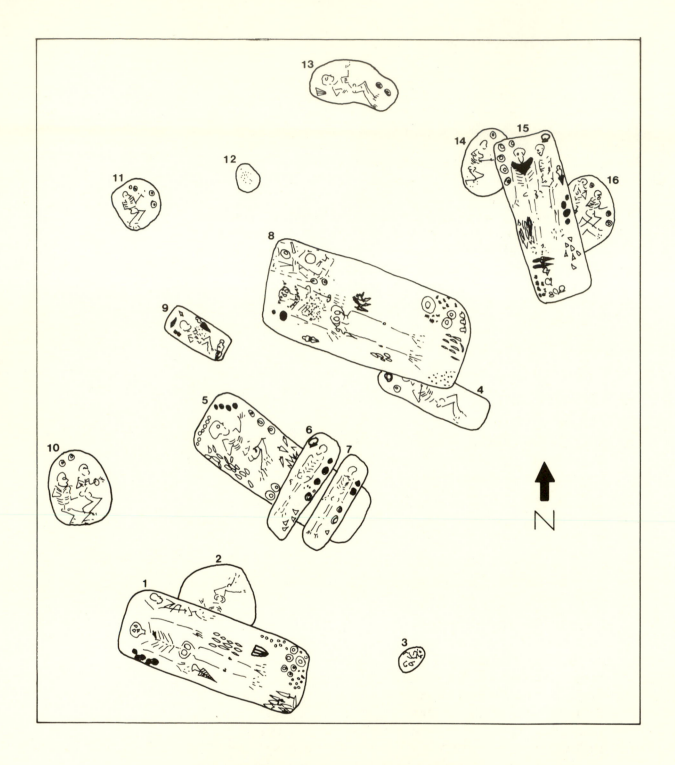

Figure 5.4. Dr. Humus's plan of the cemetery.

10. Double burial. Male, 25–30 years. Female, mid-20s. Offerings: 2 coarse jars positioned near the female, and one bone arm ring worn by the male.

11. Female, 24–27 years. Four coarse jars.

12. Scattered bones of an infant in a shallow pit.

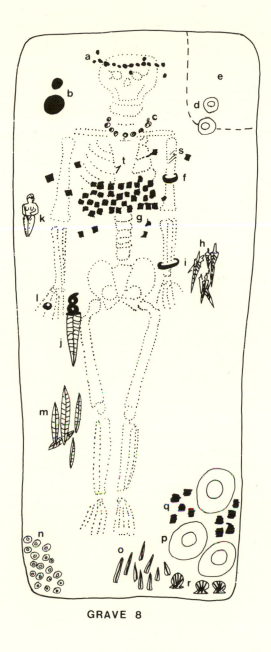

GRAVE 8

Figure 5.5. Humus's plan of grave B.

13. Male, mid-40s. Offerings: 2 rounded pebbles (hammerstones?) and one obsidian blade core. Bones of left hand show healed fractures of some phalanges. Evidence of arthritis on post-cranial skeleton.

14. Male (?), early 30s. One coarse pot.

15. Double burial. Male, late 40s. Female, about 40? Offerings include: 4 painted jars; 23 obsidian daggers; 7 lumps of lapis lazuli; 5 large sea shells; 2 flint daggers with ivory handles; 1 large chest ornament

of beaten native gold (positioned on male). The following items were associated with the female: 1 sea shell filled with coloring matter; 1 soft stone female figurine; 4 obsidian mirrors; 7 spindle whorls.

16. Two burials in one pit. Male, about 40. Offerings: 2 coarse jars. This was apparently the last interment. The bones of the first, a man in his mid-30s, had been disturbed by the second burial. Offerings: 1 large bone bead.

Something about these burials makes me feel uneasy . . .

(The catalogue breaks off abruptly—E.M.)

Submit the report requested by Mr. Milquetoast, paying special attention to the questions posed in the final paragraph of his letter.

Barchester

Following their repast the Bishop of Barchester, Dr. Proudie, led the dinner party through a fine old door to the sheltered garden at the west end of the Bishop's Palace.

"It is indeed remarkable," he commented, as they admired the hollyhocks, "that Bishops and their guests have taken their leisure in this pleasant garden for so many centuries."

Even this innocuous remark, carefully prepared to give no offence to any of the strong-willed clergy by whom he was surrounded, became a cause of some dispute.

"Why, my dear Lord Bishop," interjected Eleanor Bold, "you must have heard of the diggings undertaken by Dr. Grantly while his father was the incumbent. Indeed, less than ten years ago this garden was completely uprooted by workmen hired to find relics of the earlier bishops."

"Surely those relics are most aptly displayed in our own cathedral," responded Mr. Slope. "I have made some small study of the fabric of that great edifice. At its east end the small windows set in their rounded arches must be the work of the conquering Normans, while the soaring pointed arches of the nave indicate a later Gothic addition."

Dr. Grantly turned reluctantly to the participants in this exchange. "The history of our little community and its cathedral has been admirably set forth in a pamphlet by our Dean, although Mr. Slope may not yet have perused its contents. Documents in the Chapter House show that the Norman invaders built on the site of a Saxon church which, being of timber, was burnt to the ground by an over-zealous baron. It is true that the nave of the cathedral was rebuilt in the fourteenth century by Richard of Coventry in a gothic style, but Bishops have lived about a quarter of a mile from the cathedral on the site of this very Palace from the days of the Venerable Bede. My aim in undertaking the excavations was to discover the nature of their earlier residences."

Mrs. Proudie felt her hold over the diocese weakening. "Please explain, Dr. Grantly, how one could possibly discover anything about the history of our Bishops by degrading their gardens. The beauties of the Cathedral and the Palace are their monuments, not the soil of the flowerbeds."

As all members of the little party now turned to Dr. Grantly, he felt obliged to explain his earlier behaviour, which had in fact excited considerable comment some years previously when he had returned from Oxford to begin his duties in his late father's diocese.

"I took as my inspiration the work of Sir Charles Lyell, who believes that all the features of the earth from the mightiest peak to the narrowest defile are the work of physical forces which are shaping our land even today. When digging below this garden my workmen uncovered such a strange mixture of soils, walls, and courtyards that I was at a loss to understand their meaning. I then reasoned that Men in bygone times might have dug holes and filled them in, laid down floors, built walls, and indeed destroyed the very habitations of their forefathers in a manner not unlike that of Men today. Accordingly, I ordered my workmen to examine carefully the materials they exhumed and noted the opinions of the more trustworthy. In this way were revealed floors of plaster (as are still used in the humbler cottages), walls of stone, the very foundations of long-forgotten buildings, and many other tokens of building and decay. Mr. Harding kindly sketched these relics and also drew the strata preserved in the sides of our diggings."

The Bishop, fearing lest his wife and Mr. Slope would further prolong the controversy, rapidly took up the conversation. "And did you find that Barchester's bishops have enjoyed the same degree of comfort as that offered by our present Palace?"

"As to their comfort, I cannot speak," responded Dr. Grantly, "although I doubt they dined quite as well as we this afternoon. Certainly where we now stand has not always been endowed with the beauty of flowers, for I uncovered numerous evidences of buildings laid upon the rubble of others, and in various places we found coins struck by our English monarchs, and even those of great Roman Emperors, so that one could look upon the face of those known to us from Gibbon's work. For my part I am sure that the earliest Bishops did not live in the self-same palace which you enjoy today."

Mr. Slope's visage displayed a poorly concealed agitation. "The conferral of a knighthood on a geologist is symptomatic of the decline of the authority of the Church," he responded heatedly, "and those principles upon which you delved have lead him to infer an age for the creation of the earth far in excess of that acceptable to any reasonable person. One need look no further than the Palace itself for proof that your conclusions are erroneous. If one inspects the wall through which we passed to this garden there are plainly displayed the Norman and Gothic windows and doors which show the present Palace to have been occupied since the Norman invaders arrived on our shores. If one could only remove that ugly square-headed window, added no doubt in the sixteenth century, this wall would stand as a fine example of Medieval craftsmanship."

"Perhaps you would like to examine the short description of my work which appeared in Volume IV of the *Barsetshire Antiquaries Journal*," Dr. Grantly rejoined. "Whatever you may think of my principles, you may hardly deny the sketches of Mr. Harding nor the evidence of the coins."

The Bishop saw an opening for conciliation. "An excellent idea," he said, "as it will allow us all to repair to the Library."

*   *   *

Alas, Volume IV of the *BAJ* was missing from the episcopal shelves. The two disputants returned outside to examine the west wall (fig. 6.1); they later huddled over Mr. Harding's annotated sketches (figs. 6.2 and 6.3) and a list of coins recovered (table 6.1). It should not surprise our readers to learn that no consensus was reached.

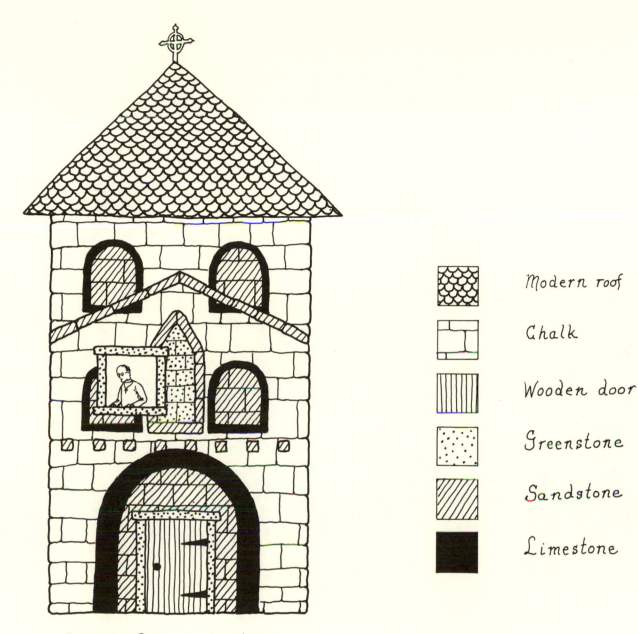

Bishop's Palace - West Wall

Modern roof

Chalk

Wooden door

Greenstone

Sandstone

Limestone

Figure 6.1. The west wall of the Bishop's Palace, from a contemporary engraving.

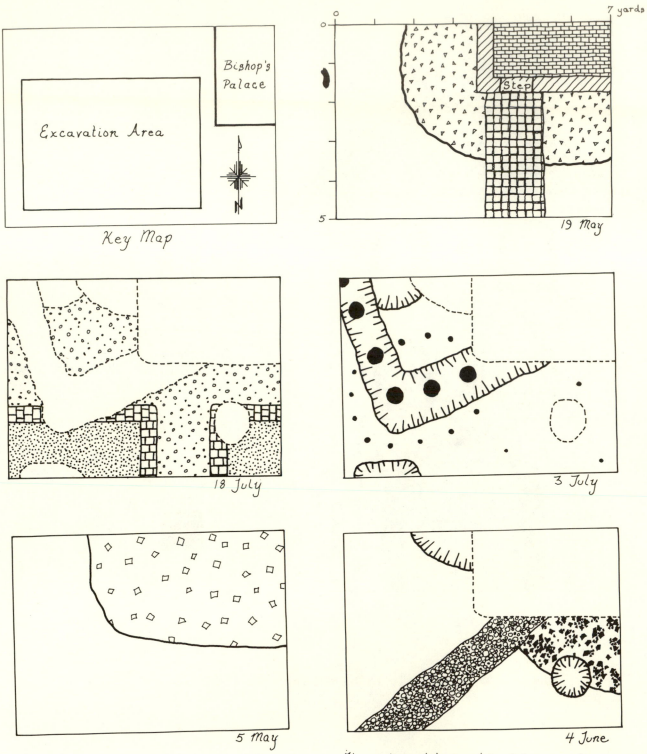

The northern hole was claimed by our workmen as a pit for mixing mortar. In the other hole we found pieces of a wooden pail and a chain.

Figure 6.2. Excavation plans from the Bishop's garden, sketched by Mr. Harding.

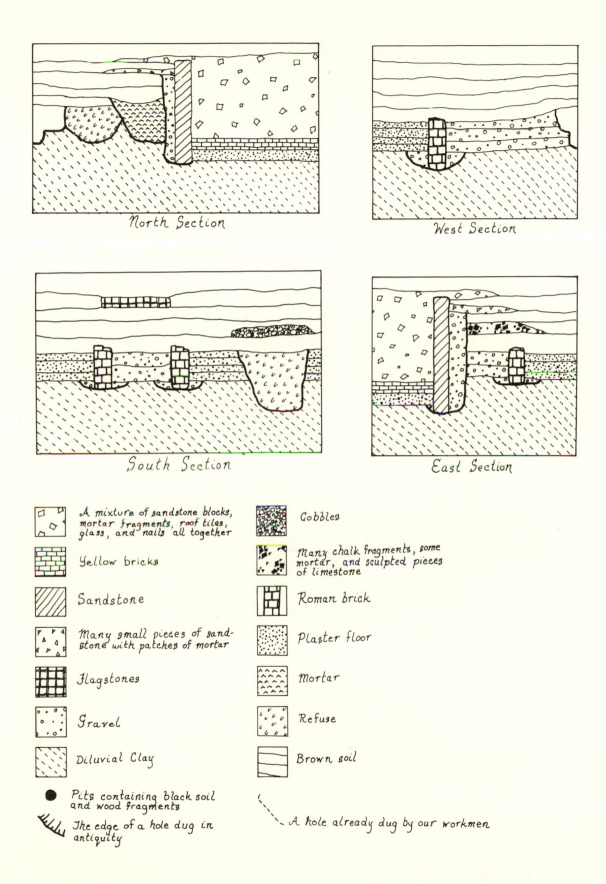

Figure 6.3. Strata preserved in the four sides of Dr. Grantly's excavation, sketched by Mr. Harding.

TABLE 6.1   List of Coins Found in Excavations at Barchester

COIN	LOCATION
Shilling of Henry VII	Under yellow brick floor
Penny of Henry VIII	3′6″ down in northeast corner
Groat of Edward III	In layer of sandstone fragments
Penny of Henry I	With chain and wooden bucket at the bottom of a deep hole
Penny of William II	In deep pit containing mortar
Penny of Offa	In pit to the west of the mortar pit
Coins of Hadrian, Vespasian, and Constantine	Layers of gravel above diluvial clay

Using the conversation reported above, the *Barsetshire Antiquaries Journal* (if you can find it), and the sketches of the excavations and the west wall of the Palace, construct as complete a sequence as possible for the garden of the Bishop's Palace. Account for all layers, artifacts, and architectural features discussed and reported by these eminent clergymen.

Latreia

Sally Stewart

The site of Latreia is located on the south coast of Crete in the fertile Akrosti-kon plain, some ten kilometers southeast of the Late Bronze Age palace of Rhadamanthys (fig. 7.1). It is situated on a sandy knoll about 500 meters from a small, sheltered harbor. The area was forested with cypresses as recently as Classical times but the vegetation is now Mediterranean scrub with cultivated areas of carob, olives, and vineyards. Much of the site is buried under sand dunes blown in from the nearby beaches (fig. 7.2). From time to time, however, the strong south winds expose portions of ashlar masonry walls. For many years the inhabitants of the village of Palaeodos, or "Old Roaders" as they like to call themselves, have been visiting the site to collect pottery and sealstones to sell to tourists or to keep as good luck charms.

Kurios Vasilios, Ephemor of Cretan antiquities, noted the site during his 1955 survey of the Akrostikon plain and mapped the walls then visible. After examining a collection of pottery and sealstones in the possession of Papas Dimetrius, he attributed the site to the Late Bronze Age. His suggestion that it was associated with the Rhadamanthys royal family is based on the combination of excellent wall construction with a high proportion of fine pottery. In 1983, excavations were undertaken by the University of Kouklia under the direction of Kurios Vasilios and Dr Maria Ostrakon. Portions of the preliminary report of the first season's work follow.

*   *   *

BUILDING ALPHA

A structure that had been partially uncovered by wind was excavated on the north end of the knoll. It is built of well finished limestone ashlar, three to four courses of which (up to 1.5 meters) are preserved. A columnar portico faces a small, elevated tripartite structure across a courtyard enclosed by walls on its eastern and western sides. The building, approached by five steps, consists of a central porch with adjacent rooms (1 & 2) that have no apparent doorways and may have been entered from an upper storey. These were filled with a jumble of massive broken ashlar masonry blocks in a matrix of dune sand, beneath which were discovered the objects listed in Table 7.1. Scattered about the courtyard, steps, and porch was a confusing array of masonry blocks, charcoal, caprid bones, and sherds of coarse pottery. The heaviest concentrations of sherds and faunal remains were located in the northwest corner of the court, and were confined within a linear pile of recycled blocks and rough,

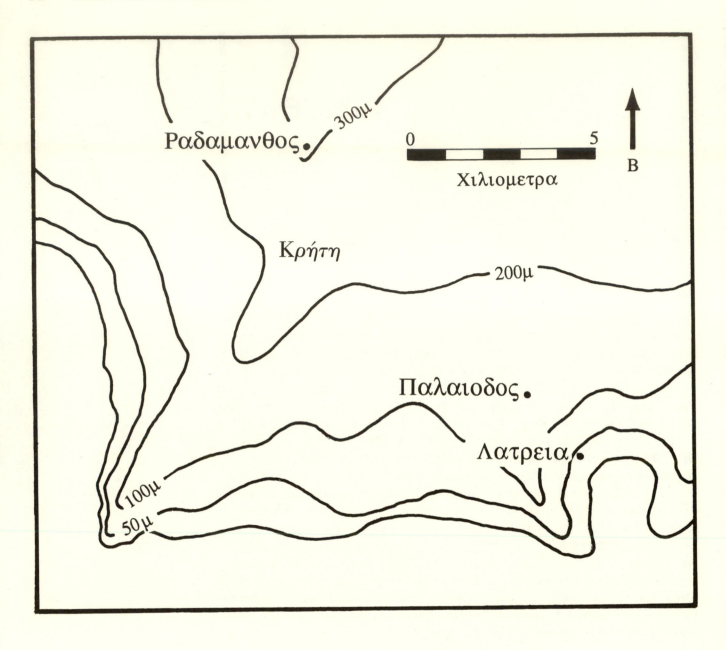

Figure 7.1. A part of Crete.

uncut field stones (not shown in Figure 7.2). Graffiti (fig. 7.3:κ) were noted on a marble block (64 by 32 by 32 cm) set against the the west courtyard wall. Before it was a small hearth containing three crudely modeled teracotta female figurines (fig. 7.3:η) and some calcined chips of bone.

BUILDING BETA

South of Alpha was a well constructed ashlar building also assigned to the Late Bronze Age (fig. 7.2). Parts of two stories are preserved.

The main basement (beneath room 7) is a long, narrow room with three stone pillars aligned on its axis. The central pillar is engraved with crude *labrys* symbols. This room was filled with numerous *pithoi,* many decorated with marine motifs (fig. 7.3:δ). It is entered through a smaller room to the north. This contained two heavy stone weights, interpreted as anchors, and various ritual equipment. A flight of flagstone steps leads up from this room to a vestibule (room 4) on the ground floor above.

What appears to be the single entrance to the building is in its southeast corner. The entrance area (1), which was unroofed and served as a light well, opens past a single column base into an antechamber (2). The floors are paved with limestone slabs. Door jambs separate the antechamber from a main hall (3) that is elaborately decorated with a gypsum dado and floor. A mosaic composed of shell tesserae and depicting dolphins and flying fish covers the central part of the floor. The hall connects to the west with the vestibule (4), in which are the remains of stone stairways that served both the basement and an upper storey that is no longer extant.

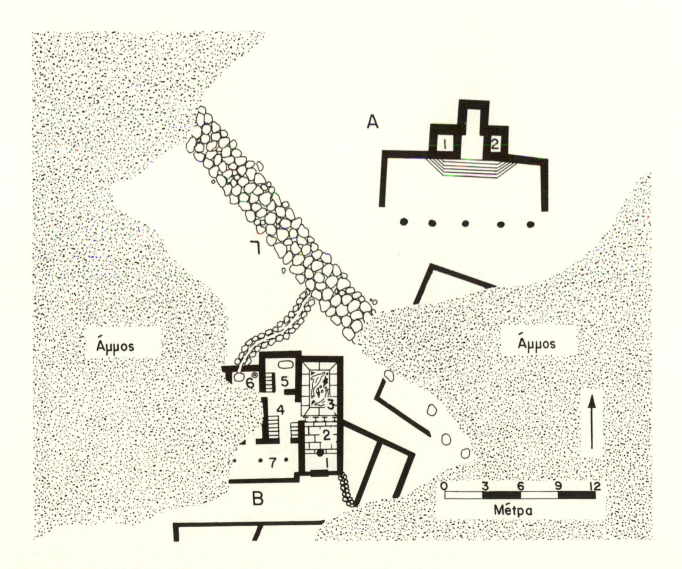

Figure 7.2. The site of Latreia showing schematic ground plans of structures Alpha, Beta, and Gamma, other walls, and sand dunes.

TABLE 7.1 Artifact Distributions

Building Alpha

Room 1—a stone carving in the shape of a set of stylized bull's horns, three miniature gold *labres* or double axes (fig. 7.3: α), 3 gold plaques (fig. 7.3: β), two imported Cypriot milk bowls, and the articulated skeleton of a goat

Room 2—one miniature faience boat, numerous broken Linear A tablets, one intact tablet in the Cypro-Minoan script, and 2 steatite sealstones, one depicting a boat (fig. 7.3: γ), the other two dolphins and a triton shell

Building Beta

Room 1—2 vessels with marine motifs

Room 2—marine motif potsherds

Room 3—marine motif pottery, 7 bronze bowls, cattle and goat bones, oyster shells

Room 4—coarse ware potsherds

Basement below 4—3 bronze saws, 2 bronze *labres,* sets of lead discs graduated in weight, 2 massive perforated stone discs

Room 5—sunken area: steatite lamp, large oval basin with marine motifs
　　　—floor: conical vessel, fetish stones, coarse pottery, figurine

Room 6—stone slab, *pithos,* coarse pottery, charcoal, goat bones, limpet shells, Linear B tablet fragment

Room 7—marine motif pottery, numerous stone weights, serpentine *rhyton*

Basement below 7—*pithoi,* large stone basin with spout

North and west of the vestibule are rooms 5 and 6. Room 5 appears to have had two periods of use. Originally a short flight of steps led down to a sunken area paved with gypsum. Portions of a fresco were found here, depicting argonauts, nautilae, an octopus, and other sea creatures. The remains of a broken marble basin or tub, also decorated with marine motifs, were found in one corner. Some time later the sunken area and steps were filled in and the floor leveled. Lying on this infill and as if fallen from the balustrade of the old staircase were several unusual items. A large conical coarse ware vessel, decorated with vertical loop handles and applied snakes (fig. 7.3:ε), was filled with fragments of marine motif pottery. There was also a fragment, damaged in antiquity, of a figurine depicting a woman with bared breasts and upraised hands, wearing a flounced skirt. There were besides several unusually shaped stones and a coarse ware lamp.

Room 6 contains a stone slab from beneath which a drain leads to the exterior. Next to the slab was a large, undecorated *pithos,* almost intact, and a fragment of a Linear B tablet (fig. 7.3:ζ). Domestic debris was piled up in one corner.

Room 7, to the south, was once decorated with frescoes depicting boats and seascapes, portions of which still adhere to the walls. Three column bases are set directly above the pillars in the basement below. Perforated stones, averaging 0.6 kg in weight, littered an area along the north wall. A magnificent engraved serpentine rhyton (fig. 7.3:ι) was fortuitously protected from destruction by a half fallen lintel.

The doorways between rooms 4 and 7 and between 3 and 4 were found blocked by uncut field stones (not indicated in fig. 7.2). Quantities of fallen

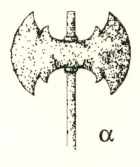

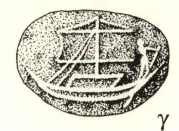

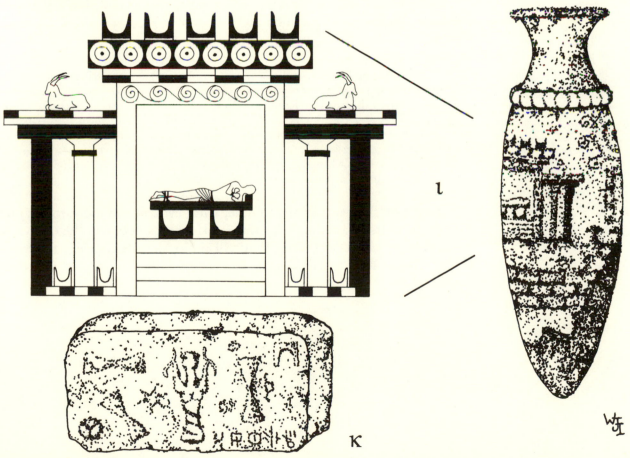

Figure 7.3. (α) miniature gold *labrys;* (β) gold plaque; (γ) sealstone; (δ) *pithos* with marine motifs; (ε) conical coarse ware vessel; (ζ) Linear B tablet fragment (η) terracotta figurine; (κ) masonry block with graffiti; (ι) serpentine *rhyton,* with detail of engraving. Scales as indicated.

ashlar blocks and mudbrick were found in rooms 1, 2, 3, and 7, but were not evident in 4, 5, or 6. It was also noted that the drain in room 5 had been crudely enlarged and its opening reinforced with field stones.

STRUCTURE GAMMA

The drainage system of Building Beta was followed to the point where it disappeared beneath a flagged area initially interpreted as a courtyard. Further excavation, however, revealed the linear nature of this feature, suggesting that it might be a roadway.

The excavators are aware that more work will be needed to determine the relationship between the various buildings and other features present at the site. Nevertheless, my colleague Vasilios is of the firm opinion that Latreia is a major Late Bronze Age cult center, which would have served the palace of Rhadamanthys to the north. For almost the entire site is devoted to shrines and sanctuaries, as evidenced by the predominance of cult equipment in all the excavated structures.

Maria Ostrakon
September 198–

*   *   *

Shortly after this preliminary report was issued, Georgios Kallipygos, excavator of Rhadamanthys, published a rebuttal to Kurios Vasilios's claims in the Journal of Aegean Studies:

> Once again Vasilios has filled a simple agriculturally supported village with sanctuaries and shrines to an extent beyond all probability. There is no evidence to suggest that Latreia served the palace of Rhadamanthys or even that there was a direct relationship between the two sites. Latreia was a typical Minoan rural settlement in that besides agriculture, amply evidenced by the finds of bronze tools and the remains of a wine press in Building Beta, a variety of craft activities took place. Some, like weaving, were secular, others—and this is where the Ephemor makes his mistake—included the production of cult objects for use in the temples of Phaistos and Knossos.

Based on the excavations to date, what evidence is there to support these arguments? Can one determine relationships between the excavated features and artifacts at Latreia that will aid in identifying their function? What criteria distinguish a cult area from one that serves a secular function?

The Little Bison Basin

The Little Bison River flows from small glaciers in the high cirques of the Rocky Mountains east to the Great Plains of North America, where it ultimately joins the Missouri system. The valley through the Rockies contains a few small towns which are supported by the ski industry and tourism. Recently, extensive natural gas deposits have been discovered in the area, and salvage archaeology projects have been funded to assess the nature of archaeological resources prior to the construction of pipelines, access roads, and well heads.

You have been asked to summarize the prehistory of the area for a book on the local history of the resort town of Poplar, soon to celebrate its centennial. Because the precise location of drill sites and pipeline routes must remain confidential to prevent land speculation, the government has not allowed access to the detailed salvage reports. It has, however, provided you with accurate summaries of the findings of the salvage archaeologists, prepared by the office of the government archaeologist.

ENVIRONMENTAL SETTING

The Little Bison River runs through a formerly glaciated valley with a typical "U" cross-section (fig. 8.1). At its western end the valley begins below a series of high cirques, most containing small glaciers. From these, streams descend steeply to the valley floor, forming the Little Bison River. The river flows east through the broad valley bottom, passing through two major mountain ranges before cutting through the foothills and entering the plains, where it merges with the Whiskey River. The valley floor consists of broad, well-drained glacial outwash terraces, above which steep mountain slopes rise to either rocky peaks or treeless plateaus.

Climate is continental, with cold winters and warm summers. Precipitation occurs as snow from November to March, but deep snow is rare on the lower terraces of the main valley because of high winds. Summer precipitation occurs as localized storms, and the region rarely experiences drought.

Vegetation below 1500 m consists of grassland. From 1500 to 2000 m mountain slopes are densely covered with thick coniferous forest. Above treeline lush alpine pastures exist on the plateaus while sparse vegetation is characteristic of the rocky heights. Of particular note in the local vegetation are the extensive fields of camas (an onion-like plant with edible bulbs) on the south-facing slopes of the Stanley Range. These plants are still harvested by local remnants of the hippie/craftsperson population in the economically slack period between winter skiers and summer hikers. Edible berries are found throughout the region, mainly in the middle of the summer.

58

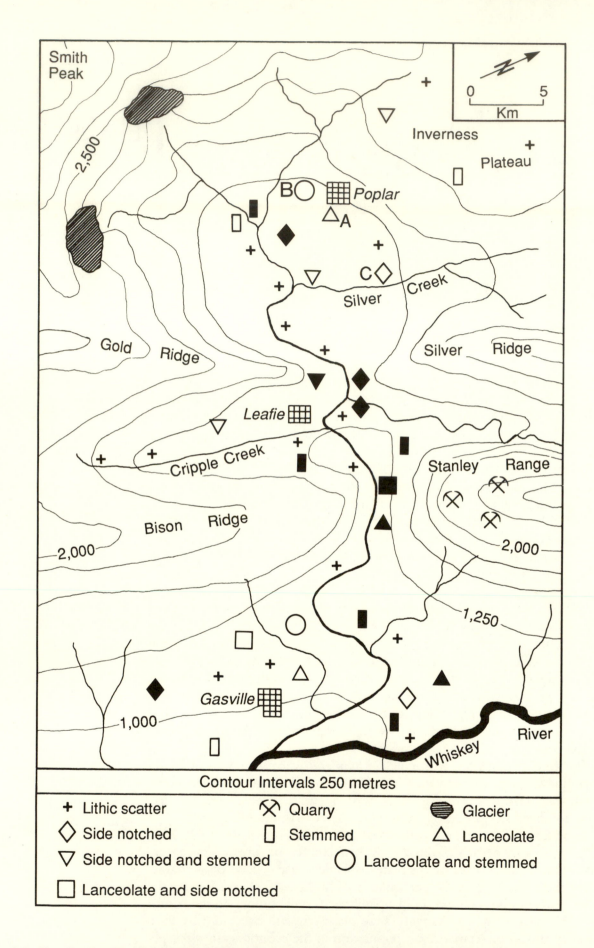

Figure 8.1. Site distribution in the Little Bison valley. Open symbols indicate camp sites; filled symbols indicate kill sites. Lithic scatters contain insufficient information to be classified by function, and no diagnostic projectile points.

Until the watershed was declared a wilderness preserve, twentieth-century hunters regarded it as a prime area for trophy bighorn sheep and elk, and local inhabitants hunted the less impressive deer populations. Bison are recorded in the area by explorers in the late eighteenth century, but prime bison pasture in the valley bottoms has been taken over by cattle ranching. Today, sheep and elk are frequently seen by hikers on the Inverness Plateau during the summer, and dense concentrations of both species are a feature of the cross country ski trails around Leafie in the winter. Cattle are pastured throughout the area in the summer, but are rounded up during the fall and trucked to the sheltered pastures of the foothills near the new town of Gasville.

Rock suitable for the production of stone tools is found on every mountain range, and in creek beds as cobbles and pebbles.

ARCHAEOLOGICAL DATA

Survey

Two surveys have been conducted in the area. Horned Toad Consultants conducted extensive judgemental surveys during initial impact assessment, concentrating on the grasslands of the Little Bison valley, two arbitrarily chosen tributary valleys (Cripple Creek and Silver Creek), one cirque (below Smith Peak) and the Inverness Plateau. Four site types were defined. Camp sites contain a wide range of artifact types and fire broken rock. Kill sites contain a restricted range of artifacts (mainly projectile points) and large quantities of bone. Lithic scatters are small sites with no diagnostic artifacts. Quarries have large quantities of debitage, usually associated with shallow pits dug into bedrock. The distribution of sites and diagnostic artifacts is shown in Figure 8.1.

Recently R. Bootheel undertook a survey of the area using random sampling techniques. Although her M.A. thesis is still being written, she has commented on the previous survey as follows:

> My work in the region confirms the dense distribution of sites along the Little Bison valley and all tributary valleys. It also identifies the much lower frequency of sites in plateau areas. However, the judgemental sampling techniques employed by Horned Toad Consultants only found one small lithic scatter in the coniferous forest. On the basis of my survey, I predict that the forests of the area contain a total of 7 such sites.

Bootheel's work is not yet complete, and her sites are not plotted in Figure 8.1.

Salvage Excavations

GASVILLE INDUSTRIAL PARK

This site is located in the new town of Gasville. The site extends over at least 3000 square meters. The stratigraphy of a test excavation area is shown in Figure 8.2, and artifacts and animal bone in Table 8.1. It is the longest sequence currently known for the region. Features found included pits and associated fire broken rock in levels 1 and 2, circles of stone thought to be tent rings in levels 2 and 4, and a hearth in level 3. The pits contained large quantities of highly fragmented large mammal bone.

BUD SITE

Located to the northwest of Leafie, this site lies at the foot of a small cliff. Stratigraphy was not observed in the colluvial deposits, but two distinct occupation horizons were present. Bison remains constituted 99% and 98%

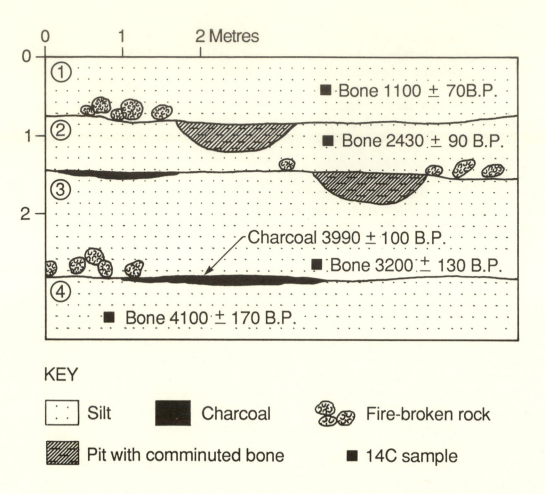

Figure 8.2. Section through test excavation in the Gasville Industrial Park site.

of the fauna in the upper and lower occupations, the remainder of the fauna consisting of wolves, coyotes, and mice. The faunal analyst noted the under-representation of upper limb bones and ribs in both occupations, and commented that the bones exhibited both humanly produced cutmarks and carnivore gnawing. Artifacts from the upper occupation included 23 stemmed points, while the lower occupation produced 40 side-notched points. The only other artifacts found were crudely flaked cobbles, which occurred in upper (14 specimens) and lower (20 specimens) bone beds. A radiocarbon date from the upper level of 940 ± 70 B.P. and a date from the lower of 2850 ± 130 B.P. were obtained.

Analysis of tooth eruption and wear sequences of bison mandibles in the upper bone bed produced the following results: 2 neonatal; 4 killed at 1.0 years; 3 killed at 2.0 years; 5 killed at greater than 3 years. Analysis of mandibles in the lower bone bed gave the following results: 1 neonatal; 3 killed at 1.4 years; 3 killed at 2.0 years; 4 killed at 2.5 years; 3 killed at 3.0 years; 1 killed at 3.4 years; 15 killed at greater than 3 years. Bison are thought to calve in May in this region.

TEST EXCAVATIONS NEAR POPLAR
A few camp sites were tested by random placement of 1 by 1 meter excavation units over 10% of the site areas.

TABLE 8.1   Gasville Site Artifacts and Fauna

ITEM	LEVEL 1	LEVEL 2	LEVEL 3	LEVEL 4
Lithics				
Bifacial knife	6	5	5	2
Drill	3	5	4	1
Endscraper	43	36	25	10
Lanceolate point			1	4
Maul	2	1	3	
Piercer	11	16	10	7
Retouched flakes	76	117	95	44
Side-notched point	1	9	10	
Side scraper	4	5	7	1
Stemmed point	12	1		
Debitage	3400	2733	2505	1911
Fauna				
Bison	84%	79%	96%	82%
Elk	11%	14%	4%	16%
Wolf	2%	4%		1%
Dog	3%	3%		1%
Shed elk antler	*	*	*	*
Fetal bison bone	*		*	*

* = present

Site A contained lanceolate points. A report on the fauna gives the following percentages: bison (43), elk (10), deer (5), sheep (16), various rodents (11), birds (5), fish (10). Analysis of growth rings in the fish vertebrae suggested a mid-summer fishing season.

Site B contained a lower occupation with lanceolate points and an upper one with stemmed points. Fauna for both levels included bison, deer, elk, sheep, rodents, and birds.

TABLE 8.2   Artifacts from Sites A, B, and C near Poplar

ITEM	SITE A	SITE B	SITE C
Bifacial knife	1	1	2
Bolas stone	3	4	7
Endscraper	3	4	12
Lanceolate point	2	2	
Retouched flake	23	15	29
Side-notched point			17
Stemmed point		2	
Debitage	113	98	142

Site C produced a date of 2200 ± 120 B.P., 4 side-notched points, a minimum of 15 bison, 12 sheep, 15 elk, 14 beaver, and 11 individuals from at least 6 species of bird. Analysis of sheep teeth suggests a late summer hunt.

Artifact frequencies for sites A, B, and C are given in Table 8.2.

Using the information provided, write an account of the prehistory of the valley. Pay particular attention to resource procurement and settlement patterns.

The Vertical World of Cuimayo

After a century of dictatorship the country of San Martino, nestled between Peru, Bolivia, and Chile, has been restored to the democracy intended by its eponymous founder, El Liberatador San Martin. At last it is possible for Ph.D. candidates like yourself to go there to carry out survey and limited test excavations besides museum research. You have already received a Licencia from the Instituto Nacional, but still have to convince your thesis committee of the intellectual quality of your project, and of its viability given the limited budget you have available to spend in the field. The usual constraints of money and time have forced your decision to restrict your coverage of space to the Cuimayo valley and the cultural span to the Early Horizon (900–200 B.C.) and the Early Intermediate Period (200 B.C.–A.D. 600).

BACKGROUND INFORMATION

San Martino covers an area of 18,276 square miles. From the coast up the Cuimayo valley to Paso de la Frontera, at the divide between the Pacific and Atlantic drainages, is a distance of only 115 miles as the condor flies, but the elevation gain is 19,549′. Wichiykamun, the highest peak, overlooks the pass from a height of 22,060′ (fig. 9.1). The resources of the country are various and strictly zoned by altitude. The five zones commonly recognized in the Cuimayo drainage are listed in Table 9.1 together with the main Pre-Columbian resources of each.

Zonal resources vary tremendously from year to year depending on winter frosts and on El Niño, the complex periodic breakdown of wind and marine current patterns, that, while less cataclysmic at the latitude of San Martino than further north, yet brings with it torrential rainfall and devastating floods at lower altitudes. Worst of all, the collapse of the marine food chain results in severe hardships for the coastal fishermen.

Access to resources is limited not only by climate and socio-political factors, which are changeable, but also by human physiology. Above about 10,000′ humans are subject to hypoxia, lack of oxygen that may manifest itself in various forms of mountain sickness, ranging from headaches to life-threatening pulmonary and cerebral oedemas. Even for native highlanders who are naturally acclimatized and partially adapted, it is advantageous to spend part of the year below 10,000′. High altitude poses serious problems in both the short and long term for persons accustomed to life at or near sea level.

The Tupaks constitute the majority of the San Martino population. They speak Quechua, the language of the Inca rulers who, in Late Horizon times, welded the once diverse peoples of San Martino into a province of their empire. The Tupaks share power with the Coctels, a group of mixed Spanish, African,

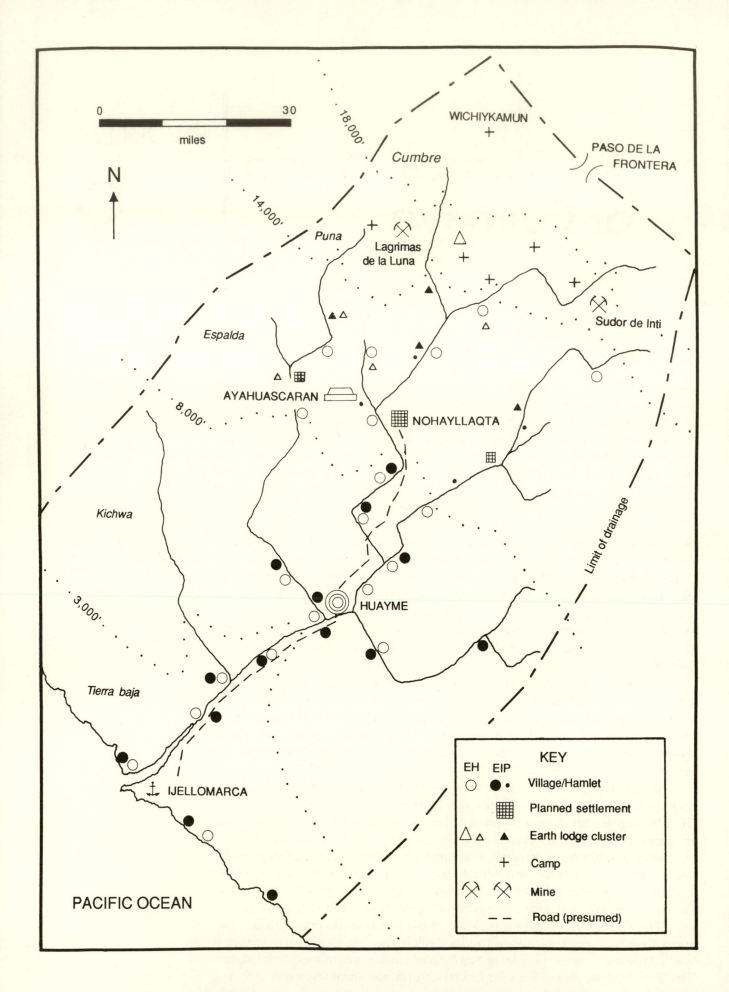

Figure 9.1. The Cuimayo drainage, showing sites that can be attributed to period.

TABLE 9.1   Altitudinal and (Pre-Columbian) Resource Zones of the Cuimayo Drainage

Cumbre (18,000–22,060′) Barren rock and glaciers.

Puna (14,000–18,000′) High altitude grassland, pasture for vicuna (wild), alpaca and llama (domesticates). Silver and gold mines.

Espalda (8,000–14,000′) Steep slopes, grass and brush-covered, above small tributary valleys with narrow bottoms offering limited arable land. Frost resistant root crops (oca and potatoes) and grain (quinoa) grown in small plots (chacras). Winter pasture for camelids.

Kichwa (3,000–8,000′) Slopes, often terraced, above broader, timbered valley bottoms. Chacras of maize, beans and vegetables. Plots hedged with Opuntia cactus producing edible tuna fruit. Guinea pigs and muscovy duck kept for food, llamas for transport and sacrifice.

Tierra baja (0–3,000′) Coastal desert and dry lower Andean slopes, all most inhospitable save for the rich soils of the Cuimayo flood plain and its Late Pleistocene terrace, both under irrigation at certain periods. Maize and a wide variety of tropical crops, tomatoes, peanuts, chili peppers, gourds, and cotton among the most important. A wealth of marine resources (fish, sea mammals, and birds including the endangered Chiqui penguin) known to have been exploited even before Early Horizon times.

Chinese, and Irish ancestry, whose foreign forebears entered the country at various times and in various capacities after 1532. The Coctels live mainly in the tierra baja.

ARCHAEOLOGICAL DATA

Information regarding the Early Horizon (EH) and Early Intermediate Period (EIP) comes almost entirely from field surveys and from excavations at the larger sites carried out in the 1920s and '30s by Carlos O'Higgins, pioneer archaeologist and founder of the Museo del Patrimonio. The known EH and EIP sites are indicated by class on the map (fig. 9.1). It will not be immediately obvious that their distribution is in part a function of the distances O'Higgins could bicycle on weekends along side roads and tracks.

The focus of the Cuimayo basin in **Early Horizon** times appears to have been the site of Ayahuascaran in the espalda. It consists of a number of flat-topped stone platforms, honeycombed by narrow corridors and passages, and faced with granitic slabs carved in low relief. A variety of creatures native to the eastern Andean slopes and Amazon forests are represented in fantastic anthropomorphized forms. The presiding deity is known to archaeologists as the "Full Frontal God" and is always portrayed holding a staff or similar unidentified device in each hand (fig. 9.2:1). The full frontal motif is widely distributed in EH times through all the lower ecological zones. O'Higgins' diggings at Ayahuascaran revealed numerous male burials, each equipped with grave goods that included Spondylus shell pectorals and paraphernalia in the form of trays, tubes, and pipes believed to have been used in shamanistic rites involving the intake of hallucinogens.

In all except the puna zone, the majority of the EH sites identified by survey are villages 3 to 8 acres in area. These are built of adobe in the tierra baja and kichwa, and of stone in the espalda, where a few smaller settlements consisting of one or two earth lodges each associated with a stone enclosure have also been noted. Surface pottery collections indicate clear contrasts in domestic pottery from zone to zone but many commonalities in iconography. O'Higgins has shown that Ijellomarca, a settlement at the mouth of the Cuimayo, was at this time both a village of marine fishermen and sea lion hunters, and a center for the distribution inland of Spondylus that must have

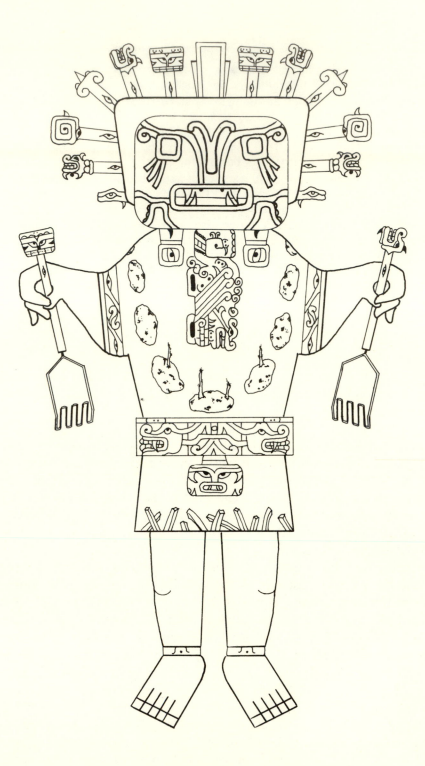

Figure 9.2:1. the "Full Frontal God" motif.

reached San Martino from far to the north. Fragments of adobe reliefs in Ayahuascaran style were found in a small platform mound within the site. As a consequence of the extreme dryness of its desert environment, a variety of materials including gourds, cotton netting, and fragments of woolen textiles and even bark cloth were preserved.

Only two EH sites are known as yet from the puna, one a hamlet of semi-subterranean lodges, two of which were tested by O'Higgins. The fauna, as yet unstudied, is known to include quantities of camelid remains. The ceramics are a mixed bag. Besides sherds typical of the espalda there are pieces that derive from the eastern Andean slopes. It is from that area, the montaña, that hallucinogens such as tobacco and coca reached the Cuimayo drainage. The other site, Lagrimas de la Luna, is a mine that has given only a few datable sherds of espalda pottery. Silver found at Ayahuascaran and Ijellomarca is believed to originate from here.

The **Early Intermediate Period** is marked by changes in pottery styles and in settlement patterns. Ayahuascaran is abandoned and Huayme, a town at an altitude of 4,000′, was strategically located on a crag dominating the main

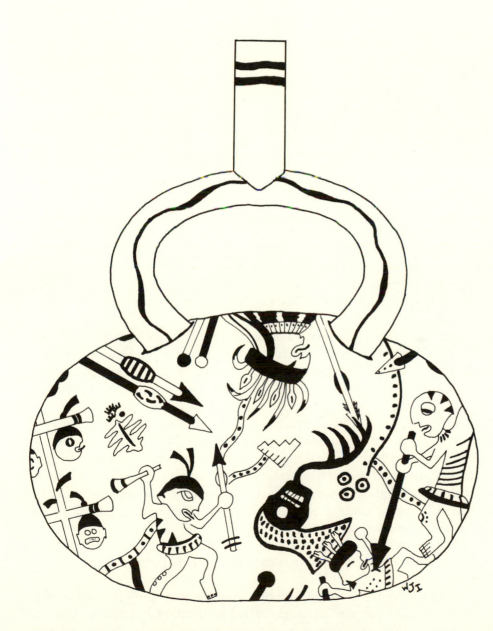

Figure 9.2:2. EIP stirrup-spout vessel.

valley and defended by earthen ramparts three miles in circumference. A satellite village specialized in the production of pottery that included stirrup-spout vessels, richly painted with trophy head and other warlike motifs (fig. 9.2:2). Ijellomarca grew larger. The faunal remains now include a substantial number of llamas. The cotton and wool textiles become more sophisticated, the styles of brocades, tapestries, and gauzes revealing interaction along the coast with centers of innovation such as Paracas. Some materials, including the feathers that decorate an exquisitely worked pouch containing traces of coca, must have originated in the tropical forest.

Near the start of the EIP a small town, Nohayllaqta, was constructed at an altitude of 9,000′ in the espalda. O'Higgins' excavation there revealed the existence of long featureless adobe structures that he identified as warehouses for the storage of chuñu (freeze-dried potato flour), and of corral-like enclosures. He located but did not excavate the town graveyard. The later Inca road linking Nohayllaqta, Huayme, and Ijellomarca may follow a route laid out in EIP times. Considerable effort appears to have been expended on the terracing of the kichwa and lower espalda zones. Surface indications suggested to O'Higgins, who never published the ceramic seriations on which his attributions were based, the development at altitudes of between 8,000′ and 12,000′ of a three tiered settlement hierarchy. He claimed that most earlier villages were replaced by communities of hamlet or even smaller dimension, but that there were occasional larger settlements, apparently laid out on a gridded plan.

From 12,000′ to about 14,000′, clusters of earth lodges are found. Associated ashy middens contain much bone, some locally made pottery, and occasional exotic finds such as trays and painted stirrup-spout vessels. Above, to the upper limits of occupation at 18,000′, traces of camps of this period have been identified on the basis of middens containing quantities of bone but little in the way of pottery. The earliest adits of the Sudor de Inti mine, still producing gold today, are believed on very slight evidence (a potsherd found in early tailings and painted with the head of a penguin in coastal EIP style) to have been sunk at this time.

Settlements and finds provisionally attributed to one or the other period under consideration include small, steep-sided mounds, built of stone or adobe, that are widely distributed in the Cuimayo basin and termed huacas or shrines by the Tupaks. Rituals are said still to take place at them, and O'Higgins avoided exacerbating local feelings by investigating them. Second, the French climber, Isabelle Marliac, while making a remarkable solo first ascent of Wichykamun, discovered two mummies in a small cave at 21,000′. She was reported in *Le Bulletin des Alpinistes* as stating that one, "était un jeune homme enveloppé en robes de coton, brodées avec le dessin d'un monsieur avec un bâton ou sceptre à chaque main." The other she described as "un guerrier vêtu en tunique et jupe de laine. Il avait ses armes avec lui et, ce qui m'a beaucoup choqué, une tête d'homme attachée à sa ceinture."

Such are the published archaeological data. O'Higgins's collections, to which you have access, are stored at the Museo del Patrimonio.

MODELS AND HYPOTHESES   Your general model is that, just as today so in the past, the production of the vertically stacked Cuimayo life zones varied erratically from year to year, and that the populations of the zones must therefore have had to rely on each other for both necessities and luxury items. Meat, wool, root crops, Amazonian products, and the means of transporting them would have been the specialities of the puna and espalda, while marine foodstuffs, cotton, cereals, and exotic items from up and down the Pacific seaboard would have moved from the tierra baja and kichwa up into the mountains.

Your reading of the archaeological data has suggested to you that the mechanisms for the redistribution of products between zones are likely to have varied by period, and perhaps also, given the physiological problems associated with high altitude, by zone. You have therefore set up a second tier of models that is internally structured by the assumptions that:

- on the whole things tend to get more rather than less complicated through time, and that

- in the course of cultural development, power seems almost inevitably to be transferred from multi-faceted social institutions to religious organizations that

- with increasing complexity are forced in their turn to hand over many of their regulatory functions to specialized secular institutions

Bearing in mind that hypoxia may distort their workings, your models are as follows:

Model 1. The population was homogeneous and moved cyclically between zones, obtaining all necessary resources in the course of its travels.

Model 2. Balanced reciprocity characterized the relationships between zones. Unforced trade and exchange redistributed materials as required.

Model 3. Access to the products of other zones was so critical that populations based in one zone could not rely upon exchange and therefore sent out colonies into neighboring zones to widen the range of resources that they could procure directly.

Model 4. Access to the resources of other zones could only be ensured by military domination and the exaction of tribute.

*   *   *

So much for models (though you may of course reject or combine any of the above, or develop ones of your own). What your committee wants is for you to formulate a research design that describes what data you propose to collect and what you will do with it. Your research proposal should minimally include:

- a proposed schedule of research in the field (keep this brief as you will quite certainly depart from it in practice),

- a description of the data you propose to gather either in the museum or in the course of survey and test excavations, and

- a statement of the hypotheses, including where necessary an explanation of their derivation from the models, that you propose to test against the data. The outcome of those tests should allow you to choose between the models.

For example, if model 1 is correct one may hypothesize that there will be no inter-zone variation in ceramic styles. In order to test this out, it will be necessary that your museum and fieldwork results include the analysis of pottery series (but which, you can't study them all?) from at least two zones of both periods.

Your committee, unlike some, does not demand the impossible. They know that although you have been preparing yourself for the field by learning Quechua and developing your skills in ceramic and faunal analysis, your budget is limited to Platas 12,000, enough to support yourself in San Martino for 9 months and carry out six weeks of excavations with a workforce of about half a dozen. You will also be able to employ a full time assistant and some casual labor to help you in carrying out archaeological surveys and museum studies.

Your committee awaits a definitive document that describes a feasible, well-crafted and astute research design.

Khina Ethnoarchaeology

The Khinas are subsistence farmers supporting themselves by intensive culti-
vation of the plateau and slopes of the Hamr el Bash mountains of central
Africa. The archaeology of the region is unknown and what little data we have
on the ethnography is culled from the observations of district officers, agron-
omists, and various other visitors, including the well-known novelist, Andrew
Geid.

In anticipation of carrying out the first archaeological survey in the area,
you have been studying this miscellany, classifying it by subject matter. Under
the heading **Ceramics, taphonomy of,** you have accumulated the following.

1. From a report "Fersiallitic soils of the Hamr and their potential," by
Jean Courge:

> One is constantly stumbling over old pots with broken bottoms. These are filled
> with moist leaf litter and set out in the fields to trap the termites that they feed their
> scrawny chickens.

2. From a note in the *Centrafrican Field,* vol. 14, 1922, by Miss A.
Solemnis, a missionary teacher of home economics who had taken her pupils
on a field trip to the Khina hills:

> . . . such lovely country, and such tall upstanding, well-formed people. As we
> climbed up to the village we breasted a stream of women and children, very colourful with
> their ochre-stained bodies and red and yellow beads, off to the well with water pots poised
> on their heads—though the steep track bore testimony to occasional accidents. Their
> flashing smiles gave us welcome. After greeting the chief, my girls sketched a family
> compound and its furnishings (fig. 10.1), and one of the imposing Khina granaries (fig.
> 10.2). The household was well-appointed with privy and corner for ablutions. Rubbish is
> tossed onto a midden and incorporated little by little into the home fields.
>
> I had selected the residence of a monogamous family for this study, but had not
> realised quite how much even the younger Khina are still slaves to superstition. Many of
> their pots are a health hazard, smeared with blood and other pungent relicts of the goats
> and chickens slaughtered in their rites. Those so besmirched sported odd spikes and other
> excrescences. The cooking pots on the other hand are finely made though blackened by
> use. Other vessels, bowls, serving dishes and the like, were admirably polished and of a
> reddish colour (fig. 10.3).
>
> One group of girls was told off to enquire into the cost of pottery. A medium sized
> vessel can be acquired for the eighth of one of the locally smelted iron bars or for half a
> peck of grain. The pots put to the fire break and must be replaced every two years or so,
> serving dishes and bowls surviving rather longer. All these they take with them if they
> move house, together with the great storage jars that may last a generation. Should there
> be a death in the family, the grave of a man is marked by his meat pot, that of a woman by

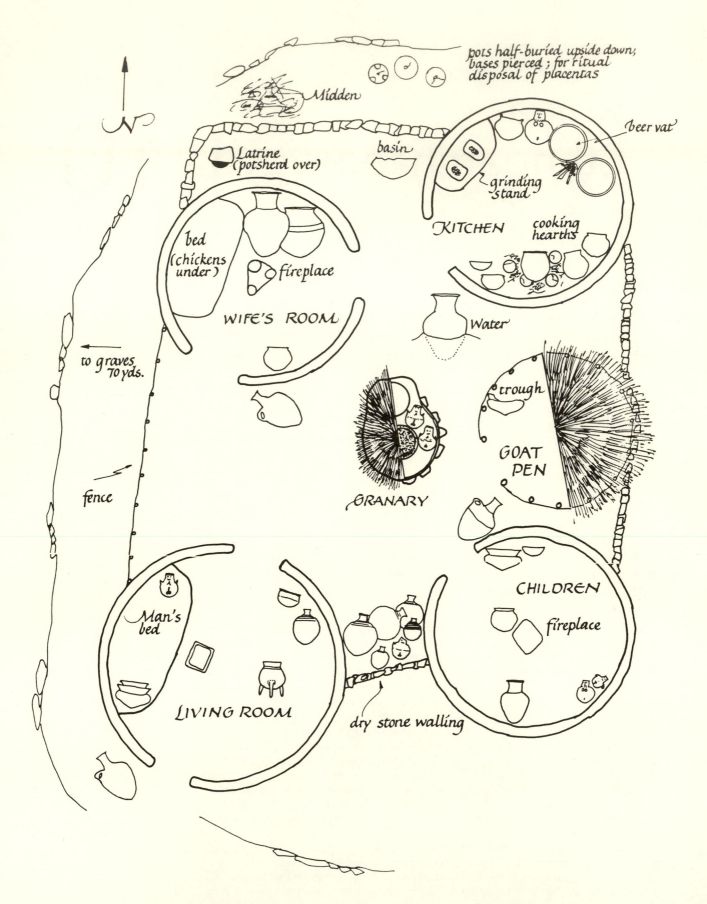

Figure 10.1. Sketch plan of a Khina compound, showing pottery and built-in furnishings. Not to scale.

Figure 10.2. A Khina granary in cross section, with fetish pots.

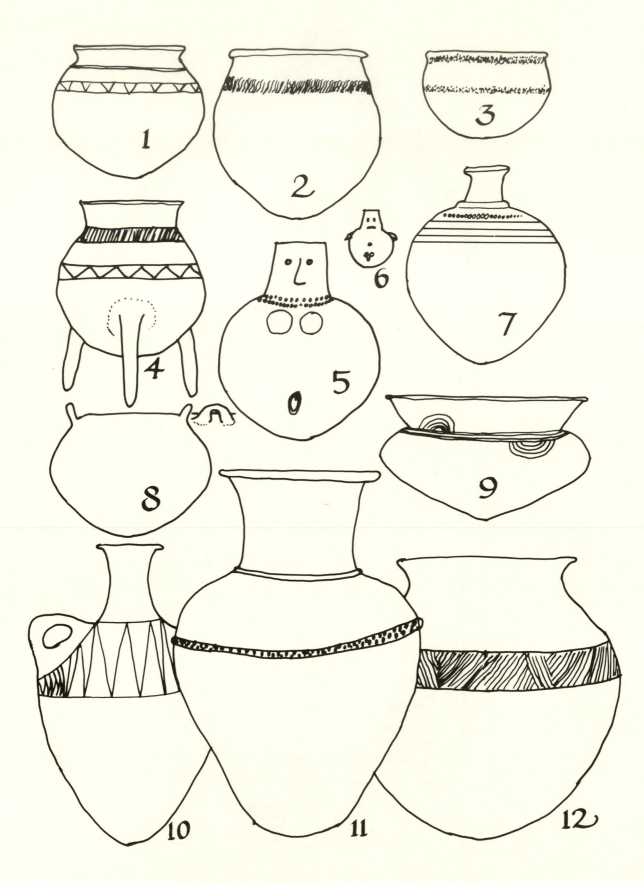

Figure 10.3. Khina pottery. (1,2) cook pots; (3) bowl; (4) man's meat pot; (5,6) woman's and child's fetish pots; (7) beer jug; (8) flour pot; (9) serving dish; (10) water jug; (11) storage jar; (12) beer vat/storage jar.

the vessel in which she was used to store flour. Most of the articles lasting ten or more years are, paradoxically, the worst made: the fetish pots hidden in various corners and brought out only on occasions. If any pot cracks or breaks it may yet be used for whatever task it or its fragments are apt. The Khina waste not even if, sad to say, they sometimes want.

We were struck by the cleanliness and obvious happiness of this hilltop people. Had we been born Khina, we would not have wished to leave.

3. From *Purple Passages* (Brighton, 1923) by A. Geid:

In the evening after the boys had raised my Egyptian tent, I talked through my faithful Abdu with Badagay, an elder of the Keenas whose intellectual powers became steadily more apparent as a crescent moon traced its limpid path across a crystalline heaven.

A.G.: Tell me of your gods.

B.: Gods! We have but one, who is both everywhere and nowhere, for She is never seen. But sparks of Her are in all of us, one in the body and one extracorporeal to which we however give a resting place.

A.G.: And what might that place be?

B.: Why men are but clay and live in huts of clay. So do we offer pots for our souls to rest in when they will, and for those other beings who both protect and trouble us, the Lord Guineacorn and Twinspirit.

A.G.: And do they stay there?

B.: No, for these are free spirits who go where they will. But we may call them with sacrifice, placing a little meat on a sherd and laying it on the paths leading to the four corners. Then they come and we speak with them. But with our fathers we may always speak.

A.G.: And how can that be?

B.: When a man leaves this world one spark is reunited with She, the great one, the other remains a while among the family, finding a lodging in the pots we guard in the upper granary. We talk with them, seeking their advice and accepting their chastisement for things illdone or undone.

A.G.: (aside) Veritable telephones to the beyond! (and to Badagay) You are then so foolish as to worship your ancestors?

B.: They are our fathers and our mothers who gave us life and land; should we not respect them? Tell me, man-who-wraps-his-legs-in-cowhide (for so he addressed me, not formerly having seen safari boots), where are your chieftains buried?

A.G.: Why in Westminster Abbey, in splendid tombs upon which they lie carved in effigy. Frightfully moving, really, the services.

B.: So that all may know the line from which they and your nation are sprung?

A.G.: Why golly gosh, I suppose so, yes.

B.: I see that you are as we, but know not what you do. My friend, stay with us for enlightenment.

Badagay then called for a jug of beer. It arrived in a coarsely made pot sporting the features and crudely moulded genitalia of a man. When I asked him what this might signify he replied that this pot had once held the soul of his father. Climbing into the granary one morning, he had fallen against it and chipped its lip. As soon as a new, pristine abode for the divine spark had been supplied by a potter, this imperfect vessel had, as is customary, been demoted to a vulgar purpose.

4. From District Officer Patrice Borgne's notes for a Trek Report (National Archives mss. 3m.ta3.1918).

These bloody people won't keep still when you want them to and won't budge when you try and move them. When the head of the family dies they up and leave the compound, abandoning half their stuff. The eldest son then rebuilds, but nearby and not in the fertile lowlands, and puts himself to quite unnecessary expense by furnishing the homestead with a new set of juju pots.

*   *   *

According to Patricia Rice (*Pottery Analysis,* Chicago, 1987),

> If a pot is found in a burial or a cache, or on a living surface in association with a cooking fire or with its contents intact, the function of the vessel—at least at the time it became a part of the archaeological record—is fairly clear.

Is this in fact the case among the Khinas? What are the cultural processes affecting ceramics that are at work in the formation of the Khina archaeological record? Show how, as a product of these processes, ceramic inventories in occupied and abandoned Khina compounds are likely to differ. Then describe in general terms the pattern of distribution of ceramics across a Khina village landscape that would be found archaeologically.

You may wish to consider the implications of the above for archaeological research design. Alternatively, how would your findings differ amongst that section of the Khina that has recently converted to Christianity, or among those near the border who, enriched by smuggling, are now purchasing many pottery substitutes while remaining faithful to their traditional beliefs?

Earp County

The boundary between the American Southwest and the Plains culture areas lies somewhere between the easternmost mountain ranges of New Mexico and the plains grasslands of western Texas. Earp County straddles this transition. Dr. A. Oakley II, the new director of the Steertown Cultural Center and Cattle Museum, is embroiled in a controversy with the Museum's trustees over her plans to spend this year's budget on a new prehistory gallery, rather than mounting an exhibition on the Earp County Cattle Wars. The director claims that the current prehistory gallery, entitled "The Pueblo Massacres," misrepresents Native American later prehistory as too violent. The trustees cite the classic monograph "Excavations at the Tunstall Ruin" (by Alfredo Badin, School of Southwestern Research, 1936) as evidence that the later prehistory of the region was characterized by incessant warfare between sedentary horticulturalists to the west and nomadic bison hunters to the east, culminating in the massacre of Pueblo groups and the withdrawal of survivors further west.

To resolve this dispute, you have been hired as an impartial consultant to review the archaeological evidence from the county, and to present an up-to-date view of the later prehistory of the area. The following information has been sent to you.

EARP COUNTY

Earp County runs from the heights of the Diego Mountains in the west to the border of Texas in the east (fig. 11.1). Vegetation is zoned altitudinally. Pine forests clothe the mountain slopes. These give way to piñon-juniper forests along the foothills, which are replaced by dry grasslands throughout the rest of the county. Major faunal species include deer and cottontail in the forested regions and along the river and stream valleys, and pronghorn antelope and jackrabbit in the grasslands. Bison are not known to have crossed the Rio Seco, but did inhabit the grasslands to the east of the river valley. Rainfall is highest in the mountains, and runoff results in permanent streams in the piñon-juniper zone. However, these streams only run seasonally to the Rio Seco. The combination of alluvial deposits and water would have allowed maize horticulture in the piñon-juniper zone, but agricultural products could not have been grown in other areas without irrigation, for which there is no evidence.

Mineral resources include clays throughout the region, a variety of metamorphic rocks and turquoise in the Diego Mountains, and El Palacio chert in the Rio Seco valley.

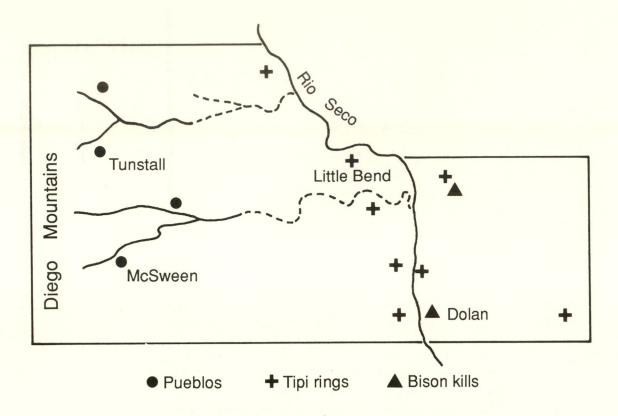

Figure 11.1. Earp County.

ARCHAEOLOGY

The Tunstall Site

The Tunstall Site was excavated by Badin in the 1930s. Excavations exposed parts of a pueblo, estimated to contain 150 rooms and two kivas. Badin was mainly interested in describing artifacts from the site, and in establishing a chronology based on comparisons of pottery styles with assemblages from pueblos to the west. Using dendrochronology and pottery cross-dating, he estimated that the pueblo was constructed at about 1200 A.D., and abandoned at about 1400 A.D. He suggested that the pueblo inhabitants were constantly at war with Plains hunters, and that the pueblo was abandoned when groups from the east massacred the pueblo population. Evidence for this was the presence of chipped stone arrowheads associated with skeletons from the site, and the fact that some rooms had been burnt.

Badin described the more obvious lithic and bone artifacts, but spent most of his report discussing pottery. The only lithics described in detail are projectile points. Badin recognized three types of arrowheads. Chisum points are poorly made, with wide side notches and convex blade margins. Badin suggested that these were made by the inhabitants of the pueblo. Bonney points and Garrett points had already been defined from surface sites in the Rio Seco valley. These points have finely made basal and/or side notches, with straight blade margins. Badin suggested that these points were shot into the pueblo during raids by hunter-gatherer "warriors" from the east. The presence of such points in association with skeletons in the pueblo was used as evidence for warfare. All projectile points were made of El Palacio chert.

Numerous pottery types were discussed. However, most types were represented by a few sherds, and considered as "trade wares" from the north and west. More than 90% of the sherds analyzed derived from three types presumed to have been made at the pueblo. Tunstall Corrugated is a coarse undecorated pottery, comprising about 60% of the assemblage. It is thought to have been used mainly for cooking. Diego Black-on-White is a light gray pottery painted after firing with geometric designs of black organic paints on a white background. Complete Diego Black-on-White vessels were often recovered from graves and room floors. A number of Diego vessels from house floors contained maize or other seeds such as piñon nuts. Diego sherds composed about 25% of the assemblage. San Antonio Red-on-Buff was the most finely made of all vessels, with naturalistic designs of animals painted on the outside of jugs and the inside of bowls. It was strongly associated with graves, but occurred in low frequencies.

Recent stabilization of the Tunstall Site ruins necessitated excavation of two adjacent rooms at the site. Profiles and plans of these excavations are presented in Figures 11.2 and 11.3. The artifact assemblages were very similar to those reported by Badin. Dendrochronology and AMS radiocarbon dating were undertaken to provide better estimates of the age of the site (table 11.1).

Plant remains consisted mainly of carbonized maize, although beans, squash seeds, and piñon nuts were also recovered. Most maize was recovered as isolated kernels, but a cache of cobs was discovered in Room B (see fig. 11.3). Faunal remains were dominated by cottontail and pronghorn, with lesser amounts of bison, jackrabbit, deer, and turkey. With the exception of bison, animal skeletons were represented by most elements. Bison remains were dominated by ribs and thoracic vertebrae spines.

Burials from rooms A and B as well as burials excavated by Badin were re-examined as part of a larger investigation of Southwestern physical anthropology. Burials were aged and sexed as accurately as possible; teeth were examined for wear patterns and caries; and X-rays of juvenile limb bones were undertaken to reveal Harris lines. A summary of results is presented in Table 11.2.

Some burials were dated by AMS techniques (table 11.2). The following comments were made by Dr. Juan Sygma, the head of the radiocarbon lab which provided the dates:

> As you are probably aware, it is important to calculate the amount of ^{13}C in materials submitted for radiocarbon dating, because this affects the final date. The skeletons from the Tunstall Site have quite variable $\delta^{13}C$ values. Less negative values (e.g. −7) probably indicate a diet which was high in corn, while more negative values (e.g., −12) show less reliance on that food. Had we not calculated the $\delta^{13}C$ values and corrected for differences in fractionation, the radiocarbon dates would have been inaccurate.

The McSween Site

Little is known about this site, although surface indications suggest that it is similar to, and contemporary with, the Tunstall Site. Salvage excavations were undertaken by State Museum archaeologists after the site's owner reported that a kiva had been trashed by pot-hunters. The archaeologists excavated a trench through the kiva, and reported the plan and profile (fig. 11.4). Dates are given in Table 11.1.

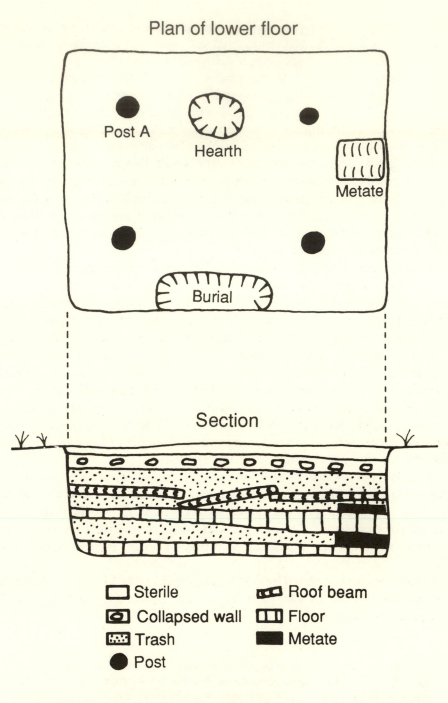

Figure 11.2. Plan and section of Room A, Tunstall Site.

The Dolan Site   Located in the Rio Seco valley, the Dolan Site was excavated by the Plain University field school in 1980. Three bone beds were defined and dated. Bone bed 3 was dated 1230 to 1290 cal. A.D. Artifacts included a variety of heavy butchering tools, Garrett points, 74 sherds of Diego Black-on-White, and 18 sherds of San Antonio Red-on-Buff. All parts of the bison were found, although ribs were underrepresented, possibly as a result of carnivore activity. Three charred corn cobs were found in a hearth associated with this bone bed.

Bone Bed 2 was dated 1310 to 1370 and 1320 to 1410 cal. A.D. Projectile points were of the Bonney type. Sherds included three Diego Black-on-White and eleven Tunstall Corrugated. Bison bones, including phalanges and tarsals, were heavily fragmented, probably to obtain grease.

Bone Bed 1, dating to 1490 to 1620 and 1510 to 1580 cal. A.D., contained Rio Seco Triangular points, which have been dated at other sites in the region to the sixteenth century A.D. No sherds were present. Bison remains were lightly butchered, and there was no evidence that bones were transported from the site.

A study of the bison remains from the site was undertaken as an M.A. thesis by Tom Afonomi. The study was mainly concerned with age and sex

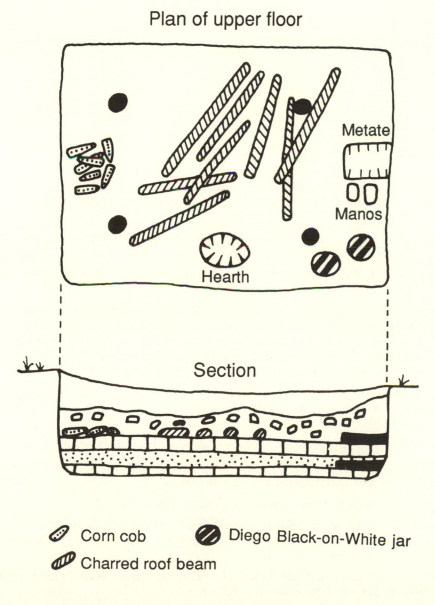

Figure 11.3. Plan and section of Room B, Tunstall Site.

TABLE 11.1   Dates from Rooms A and B (Tunstall Site) and the Kiva (McSween Site)

Room A

1. Post A. Dendrochronology. 1210 A.D.
2. Roof beam. Dendrochronology. 1263 A.D.
3. Pronghorn bone, upper trash level. Calibrated date: 1290 to 1340 cal. A.D.

Room B

4. Charred roof beam. Dendrochronology. 1290 A.D.
5. Corn cobs, upper floor. Calibrated date: 1340 to 1390 cal. A.D.

Kiva

6. Charred roof beam. Dendrochronology. 1190 A.D.
7. Bison skull. Calibrated date: 1270 to 1360 cal. A.D.
8. Charred corn from central hearth. Calibrated date: 1340 to 1410 cal. A.D.

TABLE 11.2   Description of Burials, Tunstall Site

Burial 1. Male. Extended. 30–35 years. San Antonio bowl. Bonney point in 3rd thoracic vertebra. Turquoise pendant in pectoral area. Teeth: 8 caries; 2 teeth lost ante-mortem. $\delta^{13}C$ −7.2o/oo. Calibrated date: 1320 to 1370 cal. A.D.

Burial 2. Female. Extended. >50 years. San Antonio jar. Diego jar. Two turquoise beads. Teeth: 11 caries; 7 teeth lost ante mortem; 1 abscess. $\delta^{13}C$ −7.5. Calibrated date: 1200 to 1275 cal. A.D.

Burial 3. Female. Extended. 30–40 years. Two Diego jars. Teeth: 6 caries; 1 abscess. $\delta^{13}C$ −6.9o/oo. Calibrated date: 1250 to 1310 cal. A.D.

Burial 4. Male. Extended. 45–55 years. San Antonio bowl. Teeth: 8 caries. Two bison horn cores. Nodule of El Palacio chert. Three large bifaces of the same material. Five Chisum points under left scapula. Across the chest region were 3 Garrett points. Badin comments "one unusual feature of these points was the polishing around the notches and all across both faces of each point. This may represent some 'magical' treatment to ensure accuracy. As this individual met his end at the hands of his enemies, the treatment seems to have worked!" $\delta^{13}C$ −7.1o/oo.

Burial 5. Male. Extended. 45–55 years. Two San Antonio bowls. Turquoise pendant. One unworn Bonney point in thoracic area. Teeth: 7 caries; 3 lost ante mortem. Porotic hyperostosis, thought to indicate food stress, evident on cranium. $\delta^{13}C$ −8.2. Calibrated date: 1330 to 1410 cal. A.D.

Burial 6. Child. 3–4 years. Strongly marked Harris lines. $\delta^{13}C$ −7.4o/oo. Calibrated date: 1340 to 1390 cal. A.D.

Burial 7. Female. Flexed. From lower floor of Room A. 25–30 years. Diego jar. One turquoise bead. Teeth: 2 caries. Heavy wear on teeth. $\delta^{13}C$ −12.0o/oo. Calibrated date: 1250 to 1320 cal. A.D.

Burial 8. Child. 2–3 years. Pronounced Harris lines. From upper trash deposit, Room A.

Burial 9. Male. Extended. From Room B, lower floor. 50–60 years. One San Antonio bowl. Bison horn core. Two Garrett and four Chisum points under left scapula. Teeth: 5 caries; 3 teeth lost ante mortem; 2 abscesses. $\delta^{13}C$ −7.5o/oo. Calibrated date: 1180 to 1310 cal. A.D.

Burial 10. Female. Extended. 40–45 years. Diego jar and San Antonio jar. Three turquoise beads. Teeth: 5 caries; 1 tooth lost ante mortem. $\delta^{13}C$ −7.6o/oo. Calibrated date: 1320 to 1380 cal. A.D.

Burial 11. Female. Flexed. 25–30 years. No grave goods. Heavily worn teeth. 3 caries. $\delta^{13}C$ −13.2o/oo. Calibrated date: 1180 to 1290 cal. A.D.

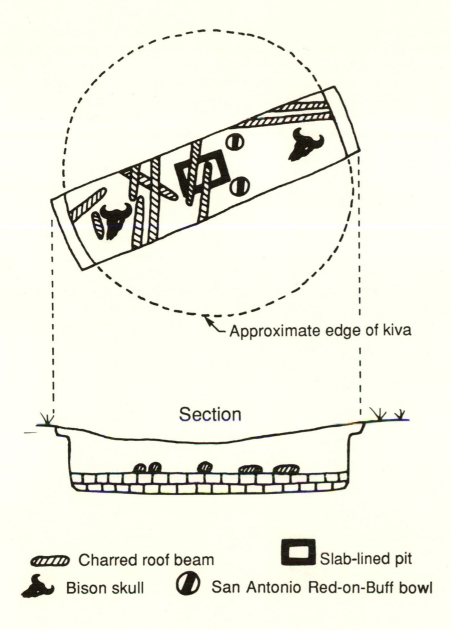

Approximate edge of kiva

Section

🪵 Charred roof beam   ◻ Slab-lined pit

🦬 Bison skull   ◉ San Antonio Red-on-Buff bowl

Figure 11.4. Plan and section of kiva, McSween Site.

ratios of the bison. Most individuals were females, killed during the fall. Afonomi concluded his thesis in the following way:

> It has been demonstrated in this thesis that estimating age at death of bison in the Rio Seco region cannot be undertaken on the basis of tooth eruption and wear. Thin sectioning of dental cementum is a much more accurate method of ageing individuals in marginal environments, where changes in forage quality and aridity can have a drastic effect on rates of tooth eruption and wear. At the Dolan site the early population and the late population have relatively low rates of tooth wear, while the middle period animals exhibit heavy wear in comparison. That this relates to changing environmental conditions (probably increased frequency of drought) is demonstrated by the relative frequency of enamel hypoplasias, assumed to indicate nutritional stress. For example, hypoplasias occur in 18% of first molars in the middle period animals, but in less than 1% of the same teeth in early and late period animals.

Little Bend Sites   Survey for a natural gas pipeline resulted in the discovery of a cluster of surface sites in the Little Bend region. The sites consisted of lithic scatters, occasional ceramics, and tipi rings along a bluff overlooking the Rio Seco. Test excavations were undertaken in two tipi rings. The first ring contained a Garrett point, 24 sherds of San Diego Black-on-White, three sherds of San Antonio Red-on-Buff, and a turquoise pendant. The second ring contained three Bonney points and nine sherds of Tunstall Corrugated. Lithic artifacts were made of El Palacio chert.

The State Museum recently contracted a study of ceramics from the Little Bend sites. Petrographic analysis identified temper from all sherds as orginating in the Diego Mountains.

On the basis of the information provided, what can be said about the relationships between east and west Earp County during prehistoric times? To what extent is hostility and warfare a feature of prehistoric Earp County? Would you recommend the development of a new prehistory gallery?

Golden Ears Rock

Golden Ears Rock sticks up like a sore thumb from the middle of Gonbwa-naland. The area has been pretty unattractive to tourists, who rush by without paying for more than a beer in Marshalltown, the sleepy little center that services the dispersed ranching and native communities. Neither is there much to detain them at Lughole, the oasis at the foot of Golden Ears Rock around which the Ortoks, Gonbwanaland indigenes and former nomadic hunter-gatherers, are now mainly settled. However the peace and quiet, not to say languor or just plain idleness, of Marshalltown and Lughole has been rudely shattered. The process is documented in the scrappy file that you, as the Cultural Heritage Officer (CHO), a Bachelor of Archaeology, charged with the case, have been accumulating over the past few months.

*   *   *

From **The Southern Examiner** (*Gonbwana's fastest growing weekly*) of 1 Feb., 197–:

> ACCIDENTAL DISCOVERY MAY END OBESITY
> Workers at Atlas Mining USA are losing weight since they started mining lethium, the heavy metal used in rocket boosters. Researchers made the discovery while searching for a formula to lower cholesterol. Genome Industries of Zurich has applied for a patent on lethium capsules as the fat ban wonder drug of the 80s.

From **The Bush Telegraph** of 3 Jan. 198–, Classified Section:

> Let a piece of the past grace your lounge. Genuine ancient ORTOK pots for sale. Good prices. No dealers or archaeologists. Call Charley, Marshalltown 981 (eves.).

From **The Bush Telegraph** of 13 Jan 198–:

> PUNCH UP AT BOOMER'S BAR
> *by Our Correspondent*
> A 60-year-old prospector spent last night in the Marshalltown drunk tank after whooping it up at Boomer's Bar and getting into a fight with an Ortok. In court this morning, Theodore 'Digger' Mulcahey stated, 'I lucked onto a . . . great deposit of lethium at Golden Ears Rock, and was quietly drinking my health when that bloody git jumped me.'
> He netted a 7-day sentence for being drunk and disorderly. Lethium is a rare metal of great strategic importance.

From **The Gonbwanaland Times,** *Business Briefs,* of 19 Jan. 198–:

MIDNIGHT OIL AND MINING announced today that it had acquired the rights to all mineral claims staked by a Mr T. Mulcahey. It appears that these are located in central Gonbwanaland, including several at scenic Golden Ears Rock.

From **The Gonbwanaland Times** of 20 Jan. 198–:

GOLDEN EARS LEGACY SCRAPPED?
from our Parliamentary Correspondent
    In answer to a question from Fleur Dumal (Retrogressive Conservative), the Minister of Defense stated that while the government had always shown the greatest respect for the rights of indigenes and for their culture, traditions could not stand in the way of progress, especially when the defense of the nation was at stake. The recent discovery of lethium in the central part of the country would relieve Gonbwanaland of a debilitating dependence upon imports of the substance from Kampuchea, the only available source in the free world.
    F. Dumal (R.C.). A supplementary, Mr. Speaker; is the Minister aware that Golden Ears Rock is the site of a treasury of Ortok art, and that moreover the rock is the *sanctum sanctorum* of the Ortoks, the place at which their girls are initiated?
    The Right Hon. Bo Deller (Notional Socialist), Minister of Defense. I am quite sure that the Ortoks will be prepared to sacrifice some little part of what they hold dear for the sake of a nation of which they are almost as much part as you or I. (Cries of 'Hear, hear!' and 'Shame!'.)
    The Minister of Culture was at this time seen hurriedly leaving the Chamber.

From **Money Talks** of 21 Jan 198–:

by Emma Chizzit
    . . . The CEO of Midnight Oil and Mining skirted the issue of the destruction of Golden Ears Rock, lately revealed as seamed with massive deposits of lethium ore. Said blonde fortyish tycoon Terri Pucker, "When we set up Ecoconcern we challenged other companies to be good environmental citizens. The real Golden Ears Rock will survive. While its massive body will be transferred to the smelters in the service of the nation, its heart and soul will be preserved for ever in the Midnight Gallery of Ortok Art and Culture. Mining of the rock is going to mean jobs, jobs, jobs, and substantial rises in the living standards of all the inhabitants of that part of the Central District. We can put our hands on our hearts and say, 'What's good for M.O.M. is good for Gonbwanaland.' "

INTER-OFFICE MEMORANDUM
To: The Hon. Minister of Culture
From: Cultural Heritage Officer, Central District
Date: 20 Jan. 198–
Re: Golden Ears Sanctuary
    I confirm statements attributed to F. Dumal in your cable of today's date regarding primal importance of GER as Ortok shrine. No photographs exist of what are said to be exquisite murals depicting initiation rites. Haven't had a look-see myself as prohibited to males. Only female initiates may approach under pain of severe sanctions. Any commercial exploitation sure to be met with ferocious Ortok response attended by international publicity. Cultural Survival International already gearing up; representative arriving tomorrow.
    Also note that negotiations between Ortok Council and *In Terra Veritas* archaeological group regarding excavation at Nipper rock shelter, site of exfoliating painted slabs and burials, are near breakdown. Dig of potentially great interest.
    Ortok Council proposes setting up a "Possessing The Land" theme park and museum. Declares itself against all other commercial development.
    Send instructions urgentest.

From the U.S. Surgeon General's report for 198–:

> It has now been unequivocally demonstrated through studies of bone chemistry (Pipette 198–) that lethium ingested in concentrations of only 2 ppm poses a serious hazard to health, being accompanied by weight loss, lassitude, and lowered libido. For persons such as mine workers exposed for any length of time to dust containing the heavy metal in concentrations of 15 ppm, the prognosis is deadly unless protective measures are taken.

Extracts from a letter dated 13 Dec. 198–, from Dr. Sheila Karminsky, *In Terra Veritas* Archaeology Group, to Chief Bill Dreamer, Ortok Tribal Council:

> We have agreed to bring only women to the site. Surely you can accept the claims of science to the Nipper rock shelter? As the Ortoks have exposed their dead from time immemorial, the skeletons eroding out of the talus must be of an earlier population of Golden Ears Rock that is part of the heritage of all mankind. Is it not a little unreasonable to talk of desecration when some of your people are known to be rootling around in the site and collecting the exquisite pots and other grave goods that are now for under-the-counter sale to collectors in Marshalltown?
>
> While we can accommodate a token Ortok on the excavation, I must regretfully inform you that our funding is dependent upon our running the dig as a field school for our own students. We cannot therefore assist otherwise in the forward-looking work of the Ortok Youth Employment Centre.

Ortok Tribal Council Press Release of 22 Jan. 198–:

> They can neither scare us nor buy us. We are Ortoks in our land that was and is and shall be. Under no circumstances will we accept the desecration of our sanctuaries either by mining interests or at the hands of archaeologists seeking to exploit our history for the sake of their own careers. We control our own present and our own past. We possess the land.

Extract from a note dated 17 Jan. 198– from Dr. Karminsky to Cultural Heritage Officer:

> You of all people can appreciate the importance of the fact that the Nipper excavation will complete our regional randomized polyunsaturated sampling of Central District. We've got to get access to the burials, which are of enormous potential for research into the peopling of our land, and on Gonbwanan palaeodemography, palaeonutrition, and genetic studies. Last but not least there is palaeopathology. After that fuss in the U.S. we need to know whether the lethium in Golden Ears is poisoning the Ortoks, not to mention Marshalltown and the ranchers. (I've always thought they were a lethargic bunch of layabouts.) Unless you can arrange a permit from the Ortoks pretty damn quick, I'll have to go public with the *Examiner*. Imagine the headline:
>
> BUREAUCRAT HAUNTED BY DEATHLY SECRET OF SACRED ROCK!
>
> P.S. Is it really true what I hear from Pearl Shallott of the Gonbwanaland Conservation Society? She tells me that the Ortoks are planning to repaint all the rock art at Golden Ears as part of a revival of native culture for adolescents. Her chums are all in a tizzy as this would almost certainly destroy habitat of the endangered lichen *Cladonia elegantula* var. *antipodea*. The Minister of the Environment is threatening to get into the act. Watch out!

Telegram from MINICULTURE to CHO CENTRAL   1500 HRS
28–01–8–

GET THIS MESS SORTED OUT SOONEST STOP MINIDEF SAYS WE MUST HAVE LETH-
IUM STOP CALL MEETING MIDNIGHTOIL ORTOKS INTERRAVERITAS STOP AGREEMENT
SATISFACTORY ALL PARTIES TO ME CLOSE OF WORK FRIDAY STOP MINISTER

*   *   *

Either prepare the statement that you will make at the meeting of the
interested parties, in which you set out the rights and wrongs of the case
and present an agreement that respects their various interests,

Or write a letter to the Minister of Culture in which you explain in
detail why the interests of the parties are irreconcilable, *and in which you
tender your resignation.*

Once you have done that, you may—since CHOs are not seagreen
and incorruptible—also wish to consider whether (and if so how) your
actions and decisions might have been influenced had you received the
following circular at the same time as your Minister's telegram.

C I R C U L A R

From: Director, National Office of Historic Development and Tourism
To: Cultural Heritage Officers
Re: Research Grants for Cultural Tourism

The Government has formally espoused cultural tourism as a means of increasing
traffic to remote areas. CHOs with degrees in archaeology and important heritage sites, prehistoric or historic, in their jurisdictions are invited to apply for
funding to initiate relevant research and development. Successful proposals will
be funded for initial five year terms. During this period the CHOs responsible
will be relieved (without loss of seniority) of administrative duties in order to
devote themselves full time to research.

Application forms are available from this Office.

Cook Valley

New Siluria, a country in the temperate region of the Pacific Ocean, has recently obtained its independence from the colonial power that ruled the area since the early nineteenth century. The new independent government has decided to establish the first department of archaeology in the country and has set up an exchange between the University of Newport and the university in whose Department of Anthropology you are a junior faculty member. You have been asked to assess the prehistory of the Cook Valley region in order to develop suitable research topics for the New Silurian graduate students being trained in your department.

The Cook River rises in the dry interior plains, passes through the Central Mountains and Coast Range, and enters the sea at Newport (fig. 13.1). The interior plains north of the Central Mountains receive relatively low rainfall and were used for sheep stations until the 1920s; because the area is still leased to the military forces of the original colonizing power, archaeological research is not possible.

Between the Central Mountains and Coast Range, the Intermontane basin runs parallel to the sea. Two rivers—the Tlon and the Kaldun—drain the basin. The original vegetation was a park-like mosaic of grassland and forest. The basin today supports a mixed farming economy, with cattle and potatoes the principal products. The south slopes of the Coast Mountains and the coastal plain support a dense coniferous forest, the result of heavy rainfall along the coast. The combination of heavy rain and podsolic soils means the coastal area is unsuitable for agriculture. Today forestry is an important economic activity and there are a number of thriving fishing villages on the coast.

Modern coastal populations are mainly of European origin, reflecting the establishment of whaling and fishing industries on the coast in the nineteenth century. The way of life of the European fishers and whalers has been altered by the strong conservation lobby in their ancestral home. The whaling industry is defunct, and traditional winter and spring hunting of seals has been severely curtailed. However, the fleets still go out in the summer for cod and halibut in the deep ocean, and flatfish and crabs are collected from sheltered bays and estuaries during the stormy winter months.

Bedrock geology consists of a complex series of folded and faulted Palaeozoic rocks, with outcrops of Tertiary volcanics. The Coast Range consists of sedimentary rocks, some exhibiting metamorphosis. Archaeologically significant materials include a fine blue chert from limestone in the Coast Range to the east of the Cook River and easily split slate to the west of the river. The Central

GEOLOGY AND GEOMORPHOLOGY

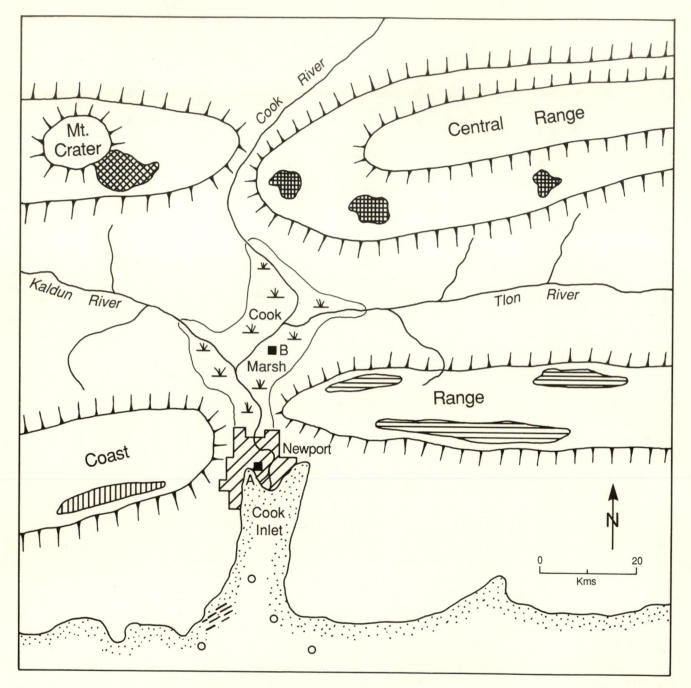

Figure 13.1. The Cook Valley region.

Mountains are predominantly limestone, with a characteristic red chert out-cropping to the east. Mount Crater, a dormant volcano, has good quality obsidian on its southeast face.

The Intermontane basin consists of Tertiary sands and gravels overlain by glacial tills, outwash deposits and glacial lake silts. To the south of the coast range similar Tertiary material is overlain predominantly by till.

Relatively little is known of the post-glacial geomorphology. However, two sections were recorded during commercial operations in Newport and in the Cook Marsh (figs. 13.2 and 13.3).

Dredging operations in Cook Inlet have revealed the presence of a sub-merged forest (fig. 13.1). In addition, barbed bone spear heads have been recovered by dredging. The approximate location of these finds is recorded in Figure 13.1.

ETHNOGRAPHY AND HISTORY

New Siluria was first recorded in written records by Captain James Cook, who named it after the birthplace of the ship's carpenter. Cook described his brief visit to the islands as follows:

> We hove to in a sheltered anchorage offering respite from a fierce winter storm in which the mizzen was swept away. The shores are clad in fine forests from which a jury mast was obtained. At the north end of the bay we came upon a cluster of crude shelters, no more than sheets of bark layed upon poles. The settlement was deserted, with weeds growing over the cold fireplaces. Yet it seemed to Mr. Banks, who took specimens of many plants growing there, that the desertion of the village could not have been many months before our arrival.

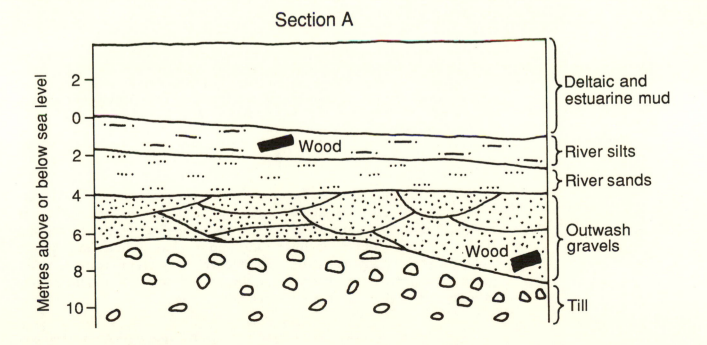

Figure 13.2. Stratigraphy of north section in commercial trench excavated at point A (fig. 13.1).

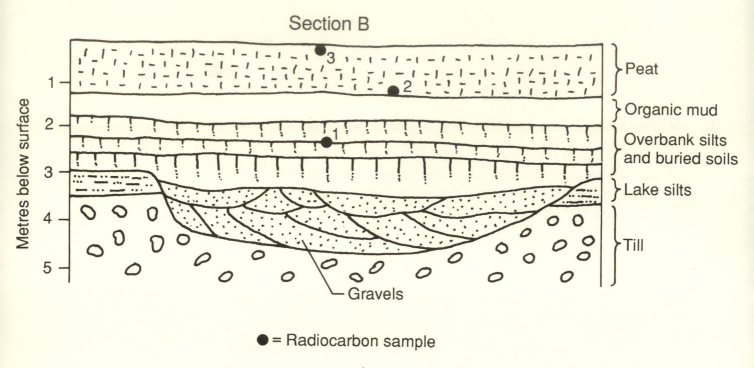

Figure 13.3. Stratigraphy of south section in commercial trench excavated at point B (fig. 13.1).

Cook left after a few days, and never made contact with any of the Waika, the native New Silurians.

Some years later the little known Dutch explorer van Huygen also visited the island, and left the following record:

> We made landfall at the sheltered inlet visited thirteen years before by Cook. Our crew enjoyed a great feast of suckling pig and a type of root which we were able to obtain by barter from the village at the end of the inlet. Although we spent some days at anchorage we could not discover the location of the fields or farms of these people even though we took advantage of the long evenings to extend our explorations. Therefore we were unable to ascertain whether the land might support settlements of our own people. We also bartered for stores of dried fish, and having taken these and fresh water on board, resumed our exploration of the coastline.

By the mid-nineteenth century the inlet had become a center of the Pacific whaling industry, and the modern city of Newport overlies the site of the European whaling station. Many young Waika shipped as crews in whaling vessels. European diseases, notably measles and smallpox, resulted in very high death rates among the Waika. In 1830 the first European mission was established in the intermontane basin. Our earliest description of Waika life derives from the letters of the Reverend George Edwards:

> The life of the natives is controlled by two great purposes—to tend their fields of sweet roots and other vegetables, and to outdo each other in the generosity of their gifts. In each village there is a headman, or chief, who farms the best soil. Others have land apportioned according to their place, yet all have sufficient fields to provide roots for their

use. At any time in the year, but usually after the main harvest in the autumn, the chief will invite all the people of his village and often people from other villages to a feast in his house. Roots are baked in great pits; pigs are roasted; and quantities of dried eels, axes, knives, beads, blankets and jewellery are given as gifts. Those attending the feast may not (out of courtesy) bring food.

Although such feasts are wasteful, especially as the winters allow little food to be procured, it is hard to convince the natives of the case. More than once, after I had argued forcibly with the chief of the nearest village that such feasts should be curtailed, he and the entire village decamped for a week to attend an even more extravagant episode of gluttony some miles away. . . .

[W]hile their agriculture is of the most simple type, they are remarkably successful in procuring eels. During periods of heavy rain (mainly in the spring, but also in the late autumn) eels congregate in large numbers in the Cook Marsh and begin, like the eels of English rivers, a migration to the sea. At this time the people will leave their fields and hasten to the marsh and the Cook River. Here, each family at their appointed place, they contrive to capture many thousands of eels through sundry methods. At the shallow crossings they drive stakes into the river bottom, and weave withies through them to make a fence. At openings in the fence they place large baskets, in which the eels are trapped. Where the river flows swifter or deeper they scoop the fish from the water by nets, and I have even seen them use large wooden rakes, set with points of bone, to drag the eels from the river as we might see labourers rake up the hay. Although there is some feasting at the river, most of the catch is dried, and is later given away at family or village feasts. . . .

As to their religious beliefs, it is impossible to state anything with accuracy, as their language is obscure on these matters. They say that the grotesque carvings which decorate their houses and which stand like statues outside are ancestors, not gods, and that they cannot be removed. Indeed, while they venerate these carvings, they cannot be said to worship them. I have persuaded many to leave off the wearing of carved amulets and bracelets. . . .

Most villagers are buried beside their houses, but the chiefs are laid under large earthen mounds . . .

During the nineteenth and much of the twentieth century the Waika were treated poorly by a series of colonial administrations, although they did retain traditional farmlands and were granted voting rights in the 1920s. Since independence the Waika have become more prominent in government, and there has been a movement of younger people away from the traditional farming areas, such as the Tlon and Kaldun valleys, to the cities. There has been a distinct revival of interest in Waika cultural heritage, reflected by the presence of Waika students of archaeology.

ARCHAEOLOGY

Archaeological studies in the Cook Valley area have been sporadic. There have been no systematic surveys of the region, and most scientific archaeological excavation has been conducted by foreign scholars. Locations of known sites are plotted in Figure 13.4, but it must be emphasized that the site distribution probably reflects where people have looked for sites rather than actual settlement patterns. Most of these site locations are the result of casual observations by local amateur archaeologists, published in the *Journal of the New Silurian Natural History Society* or reported to the Newport Museum.

Excavated Sites

NEWPORT MIDDEN

The Newport midden has been known since the mid-nineteenth century. Sporadic, poorly reported excavations took place there until the 1950s, and the more attractive artifacts found their way to the Newport Museum and private collections. In 1967 excavations were undertaken in the midden by graduate

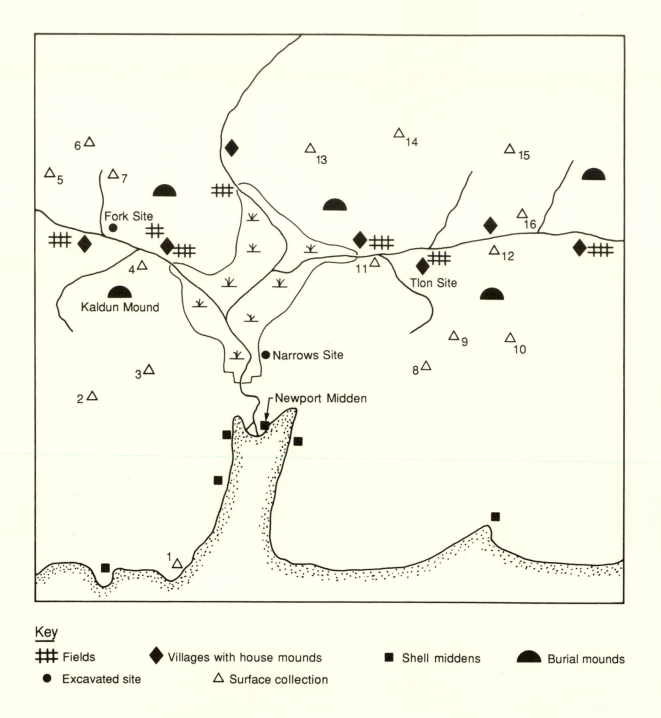

Figure 13.4. Archaeological sites in the Cook Valley region.

student P. Mott working on the economy of coastal settlements in the temperate Pacific. Summaries of lithic artifacts from his excavations are presented in Tables 13.1 and 13.2, and radiocarbon dates in Table 13.3.

The midden is located on a small knoll above the Cook River. Excavations through the midden revealed a complex sequence of layers, which were divided into three periods by Mott. At the base of the midden was a buried forest soil, containing materials assigned to *Period 1*. No shell was found in the paleosol, but lithic artifacts were abundant. Microblades, mainly of blue chert, with

TABLE 13.1   Lithic Artifacts from Sites in the Cook Valley Region. Site Locations are Given in Figure 13.4.

SITE	GROUND STONE AXES	GROUND SLATE POINTS	MICROBLADES	LANCEOLATE POINTS	SIDE-NOTCHED POINTS	CORNER-NOTCHED POINTS	SCRAPERS	DRILLS, AWLS, ETC.	OTHERS
1				1			1		2
2		3			1		1		2
3	1					4		1	
4					3		5	6	12
5			15					1	
6						2	1		1
7					4		1		2
8			3					1	1
9						1			
10					7				1
11			1	2			3	5	8
12		1			3		8	5	14
13			4	1			1		1
14						6	1		2
15	1						3		1
16				1			3	2	11
Fork	1				5		1	3	15
Narrows 1				14			38	19	18
Narrows 2			8	5			36	22	15
Narrows 3		3			1				2
Narrows 4	1					3	2	4	3
Newport 1			12	5			28	17	22
Newport 2		27			10		26	43	37
Newport 3	4					11	6	5	12
Tlon	36					43	129	84	5

TABLE 13.2   Percentages by Site and Layer of Flaked Lithic Raw Material
Types, Cook Valley Region.

SITE	OBSIDIAN	RED CHERT	BLUE CHERT
1	0	17	83
2	32	19	49
3	73	13	14
4	58	23	19
5	84	15	1
6	100	0	0
7	73	19	8
8	1	3	96
9	27	2	71
10	21	12	67
11	2	46	52
12	27	34	39
13	10	82	8
14	32	64	4
15	27	70	3
16	5	61	34
Fork	59	18	23
Narrows 1	10	21	69
Narrows 2	9	27	64
Narrows 3	sample size too small		
Narrows 4	33	12	55
Newport 1	10	35	55
Newport 2	26	31	43
Newport 3	24	10	66
Tlon	35	9	56

some specimens of red chert and others of obsidian were found. Fragmentary
projectile points were recovered (fig. 13.5:a–c). Organic remains were not well
preserved, but included bones of the indigenous Silurian deer and wild pig.
Deer were killed during the fall, and pigs during the summer. A barbed bone
point was also recovered (fig. 13.5:d).

Period 2 was marked by the beginning of shell deposition. Layers contained large numbers of mussels and clams, apparently deposited as mounds
around a village of substantial wooden longhouses. Although the entire
midden could not be excavated, sufficient work was done to reveal something
of the settlement layout (fig. 13.6). As well as houses, burials (table 13.4) and
storage pits were also found. Numerous barbed bone points were present
(fig.13.5:e–g). Small bone bipoints (fig. 13.5:h–i) have been interpreted,
using ethnographic analogy, as parts of eel rakes. Microblades were absent
from the record, but flaked chert of various types occurred (tables 1 and 2).
Ground slate knives (fig. 13.5:j–k) appeared in this period and chipped stone
points of a new type occurred (fig. 13.5:i–m). Faunal remains demonstrated a
marked change in economy (table 13.5).

Period 3 was marked by a change in community patterns and species use. The longhouses of Period 2 were replaced by small circular huts (fig. 13.7). The animals exploited from the site also changed. Eel declined in frequency, while deep sea fish such as cod became more common (table 13.5). Artifact types included chert and obsidian points (fig. 13.5:n), ground stone axes (fig. 13.5:o) and various types of flaked stone tools (table 13.1). No slate knives or bone points were found. Four shell fish-hooks in the local museum were supposedly recovered from the surface of the Newport midden, and presumably relate to this component.

TLON SITE

The Tlon site is located along a well defined terrace of the Tlon River. The site was first reported in the 1930s by amateurs, and was tested in the 1970s by archaeologist A. C. Milan. Excavations have concentrated upon exposing houses, which appear on the surface as slightly raised flat-topped mounds. However, aerial photographs have revealed a pattern of low ridges around the site which are thought to be the remnants of garden or field boundaries. From

TABLE 13.3   Radiocarbon Dates

SAMPLE	DATE B.P.
Newport Midden	
Period 1 charcoal	8200 ± 150
Period 2 human bone	4800 ± 120
Period 2 human bone	2720 ± 100
Period 3 charcoal	1200 ± 110
Narrows Site	
Period 1 charcoal	8760 ± 220
Period 2 charcoal	7100 ± 130
Period 4 charcoal	1900 ± 90
Period 4 eel bone	1020 ± 120
Tlon Site	
Charcoal	1510 ± 120
Human bone	540 ± 80
Section A	
Wood in gravels	9500 ± 240
Wood in silts	5450 ± 120
Section B	
#1 wood	6100 ± 150
#2 wood	4460 ± 160
#3 peat	180 ± 160
Submerged Forest	
Wood	8100 ± 140

Period 1

Period 2

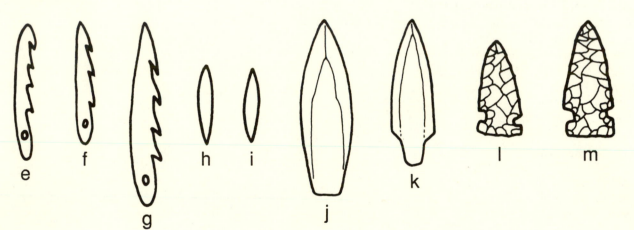

Period 3

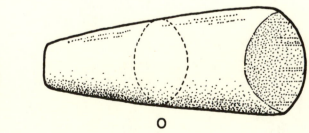

Figure 13.5. Representative artifacts from Newport Midden. Chipped stone: a,b,c,l,m,n. Ground stone: o. Bone: d,e,f,g,h,i. Ground slate: j,k.

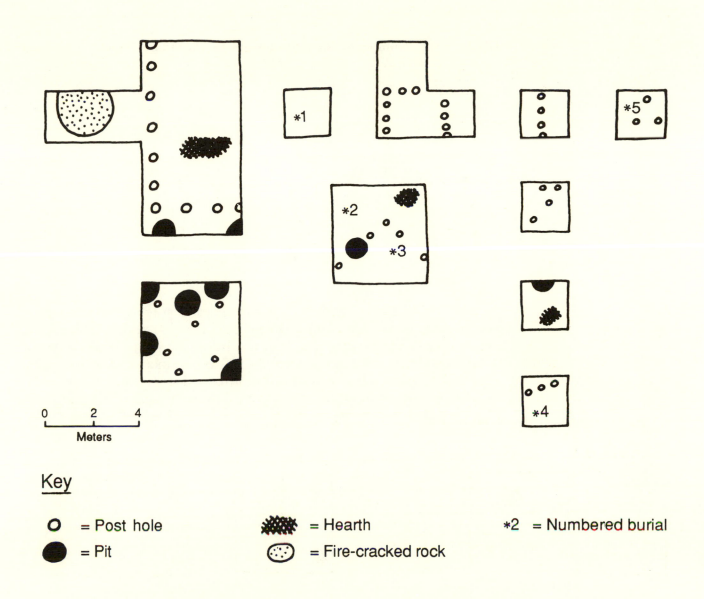

Key

O = Post hole   = Hearth   *2 = Numbered burial

● = Pit   = Fire-cracked rock

Figure 13.6. Plan of Period 2 features, Newport Midden.

TABLE 13.4 Newport Midden Burials, Period 2

BURIAL#	TYPE	SHELL BEADS	DOG BONES	STONE BOWLS	BIFACES	SHELL BRACELETS
1	Extended	43	X	1	4	1
2	Flexed	37	—	0	1	0
3	Flexed	50	—	0	0	1
4	Flexed	35	—	0	1	0
5	Flexed	4	—	0	0	0

TABLE 13.5   Number of Identified Specimens, Newport Midden

SPECIES	PERIOD 1	PERIOD 2	PERIOD 3
Deer	1064	597	124
Pig	47	15	0
Dog	28	279	14
Seal	47	950	4
Freshwater eel	0	15,348	2,664
Flounder	193	2,421	342
Cod	0	84	4,602
Halibut	0	56	1,430
Shellfish	—	many	many

the aerial photography (fig. 13.8) it would appear that houses were grouped along the terrace as a loosely integrated village, and that fields were scattered along the terrace and on terraces above and below the village. Excavations of house mounds (fig. 13.9) showed that the flat-topped mounds were the major areas of domestic activity, with houses, hearths, and storage pits represented.

Lithic artifacts from the site are summarized in Tables 13.1 and 13.2. Figure 13.10 shows objects recovered from a cache under the floor of a large

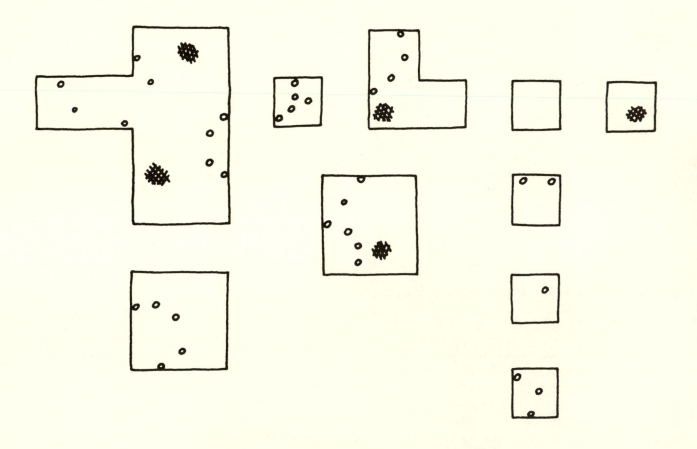

Figure 13.7. Plan of Period 3 features, Newport Midden.

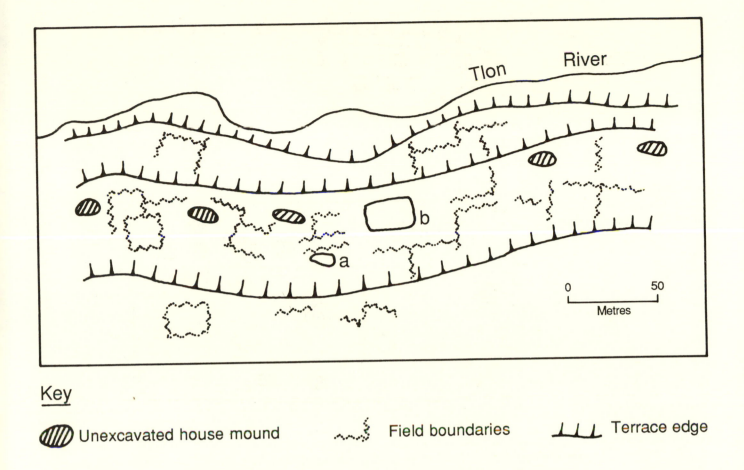

Key

◖ Unexcavated house mound   ⌇ Field boundaries   ⊥⊥⊥ Terrace edge

Figure 13.8. Sketch map of Tlon Site, based on aerial photographs.

house. The lithics (fig. 13.10:a–c) were much larger and more finely made than any other bifaces recovered by scientific excavation, although, as discussed later, similar objects have been recovered by pot-hunters. (The artifacts from the cache are not included in Tables 13.1 and 13.2.) Faunal remains included Silurian deer, wild pig, and domestic pig (table 13.6). The deer were hunted primarily in the winter and spring. Pigs were killed throughout the year, but the majority were slaughtered in the fall. As well as pits which have been interpreted as storage features, some pits contained large quantities of fire-cracked rock. These have been identified as root roasting pits by some archaeologists.

Radiocarbon dates (table 13.3) suggest a late prehistoric date for the site.

KALDUN MOUND

The Kaldun mound (fig. 13.4) was opened and looted in the 1890s by a local rancher, who later perished in somewhat suspicious circumstances. No other mounds have been excavated since. The burial chamber consisted of four large boulders, and had originally been capped by a wooden roof. The artifacts (fig. 13.11) have been in a local museum for many years, and are of a size and quality similar to those of the Tlon cache. Although the rancher reported finding a burial, the whereabouts of the skeleton is no longer known. No radiocarbon dates have been obtained for this site.

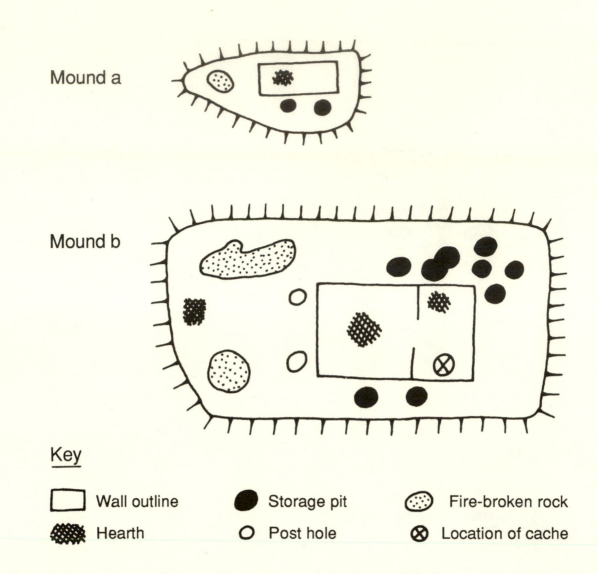

Figure 13.9. Details of excavated house mounds a and b, Tlon Site.

NARROWS SITE

The Narrows site is located on the lowest terrace of the Cook River (fig. 13.4). Occupation horizons occurred in thin layers of aeolian sand, thought to have blown onto the terrace from point bars exposed in the river during seasons of low water. Four discrete occupations were noted by P. Mott in test excavations, and three were dated by radiocarbon (table 13.3).

Occupation 1 (the lowest) contained lanceolate projectile points, hearths, lithic debris, scrapers, and a biserially barbed bone point.

Occupation 2 was similar to Occupation 1, although microblades of blue chert were also recovered. Faunal remains from Occupations 1 and 2 consisted overwhelmingly of deer. The condition of teeth and antlers suggested a late summer season of occupation.

Occupation 3 consisted of a thin layer of eel bones, a hearth, and three fragments of ground slate knives.

Occupation 4 included a thicker layer of eel bones, chert artifacts, a ground stone axe, and a hearth.

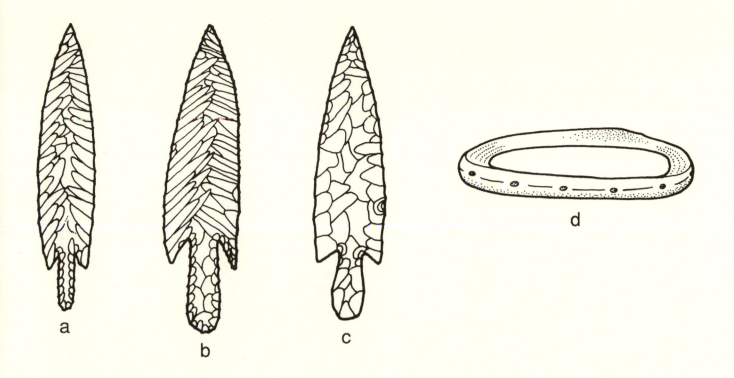

Figure 13.10. Artifacts found in cache pit, mound b, Tlon Site. All obsidian, except d, which is shell. Length of b: 18 cm.

FORK SITE

This site was tested by A. C. Milan. The only surface indication of a site was a lithic scatter, but excavation revealed a number of features (fig. 13.12) and recovered a sample of lithics (tables 13.1 and 13.2). Milan argued that the features were root roasting pits, and that the site was a seasonally occupied site concerned largely with intensive processing of wild roots.

OTHER SITES

A number of other sites are known from the region (fig. 13.4), but none has been excavated. The sites include shell middens and lithic scatters. The local museum has a number of surface collections from these sites (tables 13.1 and 13.2).

TABLE 13.6   Number of Identified Specimens, Tlon Site

SPECIES	MOUND A	MOUND B
Deer	96	412
Wild pig	11	57
Domestic pig	124	200
Pig (uncertain)	540	843
Dog	3	143
Freshwater eel	4,552	11,432
Cod	94	875
Halibut	13	236

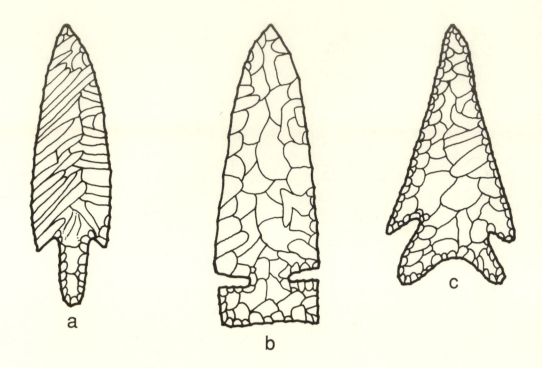

Figure 13.11. Artifacts from Kaldun Mound. All obsidian. Length of b: 20 cm.

Over the years a number of unreported excavations have taken place on house mound sites. These have ranged from weekend excavations by archaeological societies to outright looting. Virtually nothing is known about the results of these excavations. Amateur archaeologists report finding very little of "museum quality" in their small excavations. Looters, pot-hunters, vandals, and treasure-hunters have recovered ground stone axes and obsidian bifaces. Most are unavailable for study. However, *The Newport Gazette and Advertiser* (February 9, 1952) reports:

> Local farmer Jeb Walker uncovered a fine treasure of prehistoric spear heads on his farm last summer. From a small pit he pulled eight perfect specimens, all made of volcanic

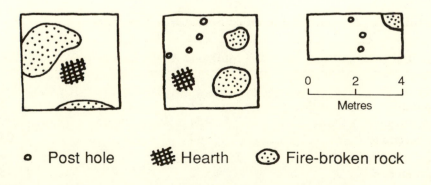

0   2   4
Metres

○ Post hole   ▦ Hearth   ◉ Fire-broken rock

Figure 13.12. Plan of features excavated at Fork Site.

glass. The longest measures over eight inches and will be on display in the library for a week. Mr. Walker, who has made a study of the archaeology of this area, states that the spears must be very old, because artifacts generally get smaller through time. One distinctive feature of the spear points are fan-shaped "tails" carved at one end. These helped join the point to the wooden spear.

This is the second such find by Mr. Walker. Two years ago on a friend's farm he uncovered four similar spears with deep notches to assist in their attachment to the spear. "The museum people have never seen anything like them," claims Mr. Walker, who feels that both lots of spears were made by the earliest human settlers in the valley.

Mr. Walker's widow believes that the "fan tail" points were found about 30 km east of the Tlon site, while side-notched specimens were found somewhere along the Kaldun River. She would not allow the collection to be examined by archaeologists.

Only two attempts have been made to interpret the prehistory of the Cook Valley region. Writing in the late 1960s, Mott explained the Newport midden as follows:

INTERPRETATIONS

During the early Holocene subsistence was based on deer hunting, and hunters followed the migratory herds, as is demonstrated by differing seasons of occupation for the Newport midden and the Narrows site. Possibly due to environmental change, population pressure forced the adoption of new subsistence strategies. Initially, these new subsistence efforts were devoted to obtaining the easily procured coastal resources such as eels and flatfish. However, increasing population pressure and the development of new technologies allowed exploitation of the rich offshore resources, supplemented by locally available species from the river and estuary.

Writing in the 1970s, A. C. Milan concluded his report on the Tlon site in the following way:

It is clear that the coastal economy described by Mott continued with increasing intensification throughout 9,000 years of coastal settlement. However, the failure of archaeologists to consider inland settlement has resulted in a neglect of parallel responses to population pressure in the interior. Here too an initial big-game hunting tradition was supplemented, under the stress of population pressure, by exploitation of new resources, notably plant foods, as seen at the Fork site. Possibly as a result of favorable mutations in the root crops, domestication of these species occurred. The establishment of farming resulted in the production of food surpluses and the formation of chiefdoms, the form of social system observed in the ethnographic record. There was probably exchange of foodstuffs and other materials between the coast and the interior (as shown by fish bone at Tlon and obsidian and ground stone axes at Newport), possibly acting as a buffering mechanism during times of resource stress. The lack of any ethnographic records for the coastal people hampers our understanding of this exchange system.

How do you interpet the prehistory of the Cook Valley region? Your interpretation will almost certainly exhibit weaknesses (resulting in part from lack of data, in part from your unfamiliarity with the region, and in part from your inability to test hypotheses adequately). You are therefore also asked to suggest thesis topics for the three New Silurian graduate students that will explore and fill in some of the gaps in present knowledge.

About the Authors

Nicholas David obtained his B.A. at Cambridge and his Ph.D. from Harvard. He has taught at the University of Pennsylvania and University College London, and was Professor of Archaeology at the University of Ibadan from 1974 to 1978. Following several years' work in Europe on the Upper Palaeolithic, he ran programs of archaeological and ethnographic research in Nigeria, the Central African Republic, the southern Sudan, and in Cameroon where he now directs the Mandara Archaeological Project. Besides excavation reports, he has written on a wide variety of topics including typology, cultural dynamics, ethnoarchaeology, and the culture history of West and Central Africa. He was the first editor of *The African Archaeological Review,* and is Professor and presently Head of the Department of Archaeology at the University of Calgary.

Jonathan Driver studied for his B.A. at Cambridge and his Ph.D. at Calgary. After working for two years in urban archaeology in Britain, he returned to Canada, teaching since 1981 at Simon Fraser University, where he is an Associate Professor of Archaeology. His major research interests are ecological archaeology and zooarchaeology, which he has explored in the course of fieldwork on Saxon and Mediaeval sites in Britain, Paleo-Indian to Late Prehistoric periods in Western Canada, and pueblo sites in the American Southwest.